TOTALITARIANISM
THE BASICS

Totalitarianism: The Basics is an easy-to-read introduction into the main concepts, ideologies, and regimes associated with totalitarianism.

Starting with an overview of how scholars have attempted to define totalitarianism, Phillip W. Gray begins with an examination of the various types of terms used, helping the reader think about how these terms do – and do not – apply to different ideologies and governments. Easily accessible language and the use of numerous examples aid readers in seeing the connections between certain types of ideologies and some forms of organization/movements in their relation to historically well-known totalitarian regimes. Gray concludes with the tools necessary to think through how to distinguish between an actual (or potential) totalitarian system and regimes that, while oppressive or authoritarian, would not be totalitarian in nature. A rich bibliography containing additional readings bookend the text.

Totalitarianism: The Basics offers an essential introduction for students from all backgrounds seeking to understand totalitarianism and for general readers with an interest in political ideologies and extremism. For those knowledgeable in this field, it adds conceptual relevance and a variety of ways of thinking about the term.

Phillip W. Gray is an independent scholar who previously taught at Texas A&M University at Qatar, the United States Coast Guard Academy, and at various universities in Hong Kong. His main research areas are extremist political ideologies and movements, comparative political theory, and the history of political thought. His most recent book is *Vanguardism: Ideology and Organization in Totalitarian Politics* (Routledge, 2020).

T0386408

The Basics Series

The Basics is a highly successful series of accessible guidebooks which provide an overview of the fundamental principles of a subject area in a jargon-free and undaunting format.

Intended for students approaching a subject for the first time, the books both introduce the essentials of a subject and provide an ideal springboard for further study. With over 50 titles spanning subjects from artificial intelligence (AI) to women's studies, *The Basics* are an ideal starting point for students seeking to understand a subject area.

Each text comes with recommendations for further study and gradually introduces the complexities and nuances within a subject.

FINANCE (Fourth edition)
Erik Banks

IMITATION
Naomi Van Bergen, Allard R. Feddes, Liesbeth Mann And Bertjan Doosje

SELF AND IDENTITY
Megan E. Birney

PSYCHOPATHY
Sandie Taylor And Lance Workman

SUBCULTURES (second edition)
Ross Haenfler

TOTALITARIANISM
Phillip W. Gray

For a full list of titles in this series, please visit www.routledge.com/The-Basics/book-series/B

TOTALITARIANISM

THE BASICS

Phillip W. Gray

NEW YORK AND LONDON

Cover image: © Getty Images

First published 2023
by Routledge
605 Third Avenue, New York, NY 10158

and by Routledge
4 Park Square, Milton Park, Abingdon, Oxon, OX14 4RN

Routledge is an imprint of the Taylor & Francis Group, an informa business

Library of Congress Cataloging-in-Publication Data
Names: Gray, Phillip W. (Phillip Wesley), 1978- author.
Title: Totalitarianism : the basics / Phillip W. Gray.
Description: New York, NY : Routledge, 2023. | Series: The basics | Includes
    bibliographical references and index. | Summary: "Totalitarianism: The Basics is an
    easy to read introduction into the main concepts, ideologies, and regimes associated
    with totalitarianism. Starting with an overview of how scholars have attempted to
    define totalitarianism, Phillip W. Gray begins with an examination of the various
    types of terms used, helping the reader think about how these terms do - and do
    not - apply to different ideologies and governments. Easily accessible language
    and the use of numerous examples aids readers in seeing the connections between
    certain types of ideologies and some forms of organization/movements in their
    relation to historically well-known totalitarian regimes. Gray concludes with the
    tools necessary to think through how to distinguish between an actual (or potential)
    totalitarian system and regimes that, while oppressive or authoritarian, would not be
    totalitarian in nature. A rich bibliography containing additional readings bookend the
    text. Totalitarianism: The Basics offers an essential introduction for students from all
    backgrounds seeking to understand totalitarianism and for general readers with an
    interest in political ideologies and extremism. For those knowledgeable in this field,
    it adds conceptual relevance and the varieties of ways of thinking about the term"—
    Provided by publisher.
Identifiers: LCCN 2022059342 (print) | LCCN 2022059343 (ebook) |
    ISBN 9781032183756 (hardback) | ISBN 9781032183732 (paperback) |
    ISBN 9781003254232 (ebook) | ISBN 9781000889208 (adobe pdf) |
    ISBN 9781000889260 (epub)
Subjects: LCSH: Totalitarianism.
Classification: LCC JC480 .G689 2023 (print) | LCC JC480 (ebook) |
    DDC 320.53—dc23/eng/20221214
LC record available at https://lccn.loc.gov/2022059342
LC ebook record available at https://lccn.loc.gov/2022059343

ISBN: 978-1-032-18375-6 (hbk)
ISBN: 978-1-032-18373-2 (pbk)
ISBN: 978-1-003-25423-2 (ebk)

DOI: 10.4324/9781003254232

Typeset in Bembo
by Apex CoVantage, LLC

CONTENTS

INTRODUCTION
What Is Totalitarianism?

"Totalitarianism" is a difficult word. On the one hand, most people have an intuitive sense of what they think it means, perhaps envisioning certain types of ideas, governments, historical events, traits, or even images of a certain "aesthetic." But on the other hand, the word becomes rather more obscure when we try to think about what it fundamentally means: one starts seeing possible inconsistencies and contradictions, finds it hard to distinguish traits of totalitarianism from other types of regimes (like some monarchies or dictatorships), and notices that many totalitarian governments not only held different beliefs, but wanted to utterly destroy one another. Indeed, some scholars have even questioned whether "totalitarianism" is a useful notion at all,[1] or that the concept is often more a reflection of contemporary concerns rather than necessarily a strictly coherent notion.[2] But surely, we can find (or create) some means of clarifying what "totalitarianism" actually means.

Initially, one way of identifying totalitarianism that appears rather straightforward is by listing totalitarian systems in history: the usual list would at least include Fascist Italy, Nazi Germany, the Communist regimes of the Soviet Union (at least under Joseph Stalin), the People's Republic of China (at least under Mao Tse-Tung), the Democratic People's Republic of Korea (North Korea), and Democratic Kampuchea (Cambodia under the rule of the Pol Pot and his Khmer Rouge), among others. The problem with such a list is that it begs the question: if we do not know how to define "totalitarian," then how can we compile an inventory of totalitarian regimes? If we add Fascist Italy, should we also add the regime of Francisco Franco in Spain? Should we include some periods of rule by the Socialist

DOI: 10.4324/9781003254232-1

Republic of Vietnam? Does Imperial Japan around the time of the Second World War count as a totalitarian regime, or as some other type of government? What does – and does not – connect these various regimes, ideologies, and groups together?

What initially appeared as a clear-cut idea becomes notably difficult when we try to think it through more deeply. The purpose of this book, therefore, is to provide some clarity on the straightforward yet simultaneously murky concept of totalitarianism. By the conclusion of this book, the reader will hopefully have a better understanding of what "totalitarianism" means: not only in identifying totalitarian governments in history, but in seeing how these types of movements reason about politics, how they organize themselves, how they typically gain political power, and why they can tend to be popular in certain circumstances. To assist the reader in this process, this book is separated into six parts, discussed at the end of this chapter. For now, we will tease out some idea of totalitarianism along three paths. First, we will distinguish totalitarianism from other types of ideologies and regimes. As a start, it is sometimes easier to understand what a thing *is* by first seeing what it *is not*. Second, we will briefly go over some of the ways previous scholars have attempted to comprehend totalitarianism, be it by using social scientific reasoning, social theory, political philosophy, or other means. Third, we will bring these previous elements together to provide a manageable perspective on totalitarianism, which will serve as a basis for the rest of this book. To start off, then, let's compare and contrast some other systems with that of totalitarianism.

Disentangling Totalitarianism From Other Types

Because of the broad use of the term, it will be useful here to examine some common descriptions for totalitarianism that can confuse our understanding rather than bring clarification. It is not that these descriptions are inherently wrong, per se, but instead that they are perhaps only partially correct. In many cases, what initially appears to be a uniquely totalitarian trait is instead found in various non-totalitarian systems as well. By separating out those characteristics that may not be as clarifying, we can clarify which traits can give us a clearer idea about totalitarianism.

When most people think of totalitarianism, one word that likely comes immediately to mind is "brutal." One would be hard-pressed to find a pleasant totalitarian regime; rather, one finds a long history of torture, imprisonment, murder, and genocide. "Brutal" is certainly a notable attribute of totalitarian regimes. The problem is in categorization. It does indeed appear that any totalitarian regime will be brutal (to some extent, at least), but a government being brutal does not therefore mean it is totalitarian. In the long history of human civilizations, brutality by governments is far from rare. Looking to the past, one can note the repressive acts by Caligula (37–41 AD/CE), Nero (54–68 AD/CE), and Diocletian (284–305 AD/CE) in the Roman Empire, the vicious means used by Genghis Khan to expand his empire in the early 1200s, and the horrifying practices of human sacrifice within the Aztec Empire of the 1400s, just to name a very few examples. While all these regimes (and many more) were brutal, it would likely be inaccurate to call any of them "totalitarian." When compared to governments that we think of as purely totalitarian – such as Hitler's Germany or Mao's China – these other brutal regimes seem to lack the type of unifying idea/cause that animated the totalitarian ones (the "Aryan race" and the "working and peasant classes," respectively). Caligula was quite literally insane (and thus, his brutality reflects his madness more than some particular cause), Nero and Diocletian repressed those they viewed as threats to their power or as dangerous traitors to the Roman Empire, Genghis Kahn wanted to gain an empire (and was rather good at it), and the Aztecs committed atrocities on the basis of their comparatively peculiar religious rituals. These other regimes were brutal, but do not appear to have other qualities (like a unifying, overarching cause) that we see in totalitarian regimes.

We can see something similar with more recent governments as well. The military junta of Chile under Augusto Pinochet (1974–1990) and the Argentinian military dictatorship (1976–1983) involved a great deal of brutality, including murder, torture, arbitrary imprisonment, and (in the Argentinian case) "disappearing" victims of the regime. And yet, these regimes lacked other traits that would be totalitarian in nature. While these two governments had rather clear ideas of who they were *against* (usually leftists, communists, and others), once again there was less of an idea of what they were *for*. Moreover, while these regimes were very protective – indeed, even paranoid – about any possible encroachments on their political power, they tended to be much less interested and engaged with other parts of society. As long as economic, religious, or other activity did not engage in politics, these were generally left alone. In contrast, totalitarian regimes seek to control all aspects of society, not just the political sphere (which we will discuss in greater detail in later chapters). Similarly, one could look at governments such as Saudi Arabia or Indonesia as engaging in brutal and controlling practices, while also noting that they lack other totalitarian traits. While brutality is a notable trait for totalitarianism (at least potentially), this is a trait shared with authoritarian and other types of regimes. To put it another way, a totalitarian system will most likely be brutal, but a brutal system is not necessarily totalitarian.

A related notion is that totalitarianism is genocidal, with the Nazi genocide of Jews as the primary example. Here, too, this view presents problems. First, there have been totalitarian regimes that have not been genocidal due to aspects of their fundamental ideology, with the biggest instance being Fascist Italy. One might also view North Korea as an example of a non-genocidal totalitarian regime (although it could be an open question whether this is because of ideological reasons or simply from lack of opportunity). Second, there have been various genocides committed by governments or movements that lack other qualities found in totalitarian systems. For instance, the military committee that instigated the Rwandan genocide of 1994 appears to lack other traits one would expect to see in a fully totalitarian system. Certainly, killing on a large scale appears to be a characteristic trait for totalitarian regimes, but, as with brutality, genocide does not appear to be a *uniquely* totalitarian trait.

Another trait often associated with totalitarianism is rule by a single, charismatic leader, surrounded by a "cult of personality." The "cult of personality" usually refers to the excessive adoration of some person, who is viewed as almost superhuman in appearance, strength, intelligence, ability, or other traits. This adoration is almost religious in nature. There is no shortage of examples of totalitarian "cults of personality," including those around Lenin, Stalin, Hitler, Mussolini, Mao, the Kim family of North Korea, and many others. The problem is that there are also many examples of "cults of personality" around non-totalitarian political figures. Just in the case of presidents of the United States, one could note at least some level of a "cult of personality" surrounding John F. Kennedy, Ronald Reagan, Barack Obama, and Donald Trump. As with brutality, a "cult of personality" or singular charismatic leader does not necessarily equate with a totalitarian regime. Additionally, we can often see the dynamics of a "cult of personality" in other spheres of life that are not directly, or even indirectly, political. The reverence toward some types of religious figures, for instance, surely would count as a "cult of personality," but would not therefore necessarily be "totalitarian." Certainly, a religious "cult of personality" can perhaps go in totalitarian directions: the case of Jim Jones' "Peoples Temple" and its activities in Jonestown (Guyana) could be an example. But in many other cases, this religious form is of little political relevance. In the sphere of entertainment, the worshipful fixation of fans on movie actors, sports figures, and members of musical groups illustrates the same type of "cult of personality," but it would be a rather hard case to make that the Beatles or Taylor Swift headed totalitarian movements when legions of young people swooned over them, regardless of one's assessment about these people's taste in music. Here, again, we have a trait that covers far too many other types of systems and cases.

Overwhelming surveillance, lack of privacy, and the desire to "brainwash" and/or "reprogram" people are other traits people usually intuit about totalitarianism. In dystopian novels like Yevgeny Zamyatin's *We*, George Orwell's *1984*, Ray Bradbury's *Fahrenheit 451*, or even Margaret Atwood's *The Handmaid's Tale*, totalitarian rule is almost synonymous with mind control and a lack of privacy. Unlike the previous traits discussed, this intuition comes closer to the mark of providing a distinguishing trait of these types of ideologies and regimes. Other types of governments and ideologies have engaged in these types of practices at points, of course; however, these actions tend to be limited in scope, time, and effort. For totalitarian regimes, however, the desire to "reprogram" all members of society appears to be inherent and consistent. What is it, then, that pushes totalitarian systems to engage in these extensive and intrusive actions? Is it just a fluke of history that some governments take on these actions while others do not? Or is there something more fundamental that drives these governments to engage in such activities? These questions might give us greater clarity on why this trait appears in totalitarian systems.

How should we go about arriving at good, or at least better, definitions? Thankfully, we do not need to start from scratch: numerous scholars and writers have put their efforts into conceptualizing totalitarianism from various angles. As with any area of study, each of these angles will have strengths and weaknesses. In the next section, we will consider some of the most important of these attempts.

Ways of Understanding Totalitarianism

There is no shortage of research that attempts to understand totalitarianism. These studies use a variety of frameworks and methods, including social scientific methods, philosophical analysis, historical research, and various others. With this diversity of perspectives, one finds quite a few different approaches to comprehending totalitarianism. In this section, we will briefly note some of these attempts.

One influential means of understanding totalitarianism attempts to examine it through social science. Usually focused primarily on totalitarian governments (rather than movements), this style of definition seeks to identify the key traits (that can be operationalized[3]) of such regimes, thus allowing social scientists to examine totalitarianism in relation to other variables, such as economic development, population dynamics, and other factors. Along with trying to give a more precise definition of totalitarianism, this social scientific framework can also allow researchers to compare totalitarian regimes with other types of governments; for instance, seeing if totalitarian regimes are more likely to start wars compared to democracies or military dictatorships. Some studies of this type are general to provide a set of definitional traits of totalitarianism itself.[4] These types of general studies can result in some unexpected insights. For instance, the earlier analyses from political scientist A. James Gregor argued that one could view totalitarianism as a subset of "developmental dictatorship;"[5] that totalitarianism becomes the means by which some societies that are "behind" others in development attempt to industrialize and modernize quickly. Other researchers focus on operationalizing a specific aspect of totalitarian regimes, such as how the ruling party in these states use propaganda and shape communications in their regimes.[6] Finally, some social scientists – specifically, psychologists – try to understand totalitarianism through an examination of the mental states of those involved in totalitarian regimes.[7]

The social scientific framework can be quite useful in understanding totalitarianism. Using statistical analysis, researchers can not only compare totalitarian regimes with other types of governments, but they can also look beyond the "surface" of totalitarian regimes to see if there may be some less obvious causes or dynamics that shape these governments. However, there are also some potential challenges for social scientific analyses as well. Perhaps the greatest potential difficulty is access to data. Totalitarian governments are notorious for being, at best, "creative" with the information they release, and at worst are utterly opaque (especially on internal functions of the state). For instance, researchers often are left to speculate on, say, the specific numbers of surveillance officers in the People's Republic of China, and it is unlikely that the government would provide such information. For totalitarian states that have been utterly defeated in war (such as Nazi Germany) or that collapse over time (as with the Soviet Union), more data can be available. But even in these cases, data access will be limited in comparison to more free political systems. Certainly, social scientific investigations can be quite enlightening, but the closed nature of totalitarian systems can limit the scope of such work. Additionally, some of the studies using social scientific methods are more like partisan tracts than pure scholarship. Perhaps the most notorious example of this type of work, originating within the "critical theory" school of thought, is *The Authoritarian Personality*,[8] which developed the "F-scale" to determine a person's psychological proclivity toward fascism and authoritarianism. While using social scientific methods, many (quite reasonably) critiqued it as more ideological than scholarly. As such, some social scientific works might better be classified as "partisan" examinations of totalitarianism (discussed in greater detail in the following).

Others try to understand totalitarianism in a more philosophical manner. This perspective focuses more on broadly understood ideology and ideas within totalitarian systems. Among other things, some of these studies will look at what totalitarian ideologies advocate, as well as analyze internal logic in these ideologies, and the way earlier styles of thinking may have shaped these ideologies. Other philosophers might focus on the notion of reality (which touches on the philosophical study of "ontology") underlying these ideologies, while still others may look at how these ideologies assess what counts as "true" knowledge (in other words, issues of "epistemology"). The most important philosophical discussions of totalitarianism typically "place" totalitarianism within a broader intellectual/historical/social context. One of the most famous examples of a philosophical attempt at understanding comes from Hannah Arendt, both in her major work on totalitarianism[9] as well as her book on a particular officer within a totalitarian regime.[10] Another notable example of this type of analysis is the work of Eric Voegelin.[11] For both of these authors, totalitarianism is an important topic in their arguments on larger philosophical points (among other things, issues like freedom for Arendt and understanding ontology for Voegelin). As a result, their investigation of totalitarian ideologies and regimes are just one part of their much larger philosophical research agendas. Other types of these studies might use another philosophical school of thought, such as that of Nietzsche,[12] as the framework to understand totalitarian systems. More recently, the works of Roger Griffin[13] and Richard Shorten[14] focused on the relationship between modernity and totalitarianism. Other philosophical studies look at specific forms of totalitarianism rather than generally, focused more specifically on Fascism[15] or Leninism,[16] for instance.

One of the greatest benefits of the philosophical approach is that it takes the underlying ideas of totalitarianism seriously and places these ideas in the context of (and in contrast with) other normative theories. As a result, philosophical analyses often provide a deeper understanding of why totalitarian systems could rationally appeal to so many people, while simultaneously explicating the internal logic in these systems that lead them to such violent results. Arendt, for instance, presents highly cogent arguments for how totalitarianism is tightly entwined with modernity (modernity being a topic we will cover in future chapters). There are some notable problems with this framework, however. Perhaps the biggest difficulty – at least for the most-developed philosophical examinations – is that these discussions are usually just a part of a much larger and overarching philosophical system being proposed by these philosophers. Arendt and Voegelin, in this sense, provide excellent examples of this problem. Arendt's investigation of totalitarianism is deeply influenced by her broader concerns on the nature of human freedom as well as political philosophy. As for Voegelin, his discussion of totalitarianism is merely a part of his wide-ranging philosophical system. As a result, he argues that the dynamics of totalitarianism originated many centuries ago (with particular focus on Joachim of Fiore, who lived in the late twelfth century). As both of these authors talk about totalitarianism in the context of their own philosophical systems, a reader trying to comprehend their arguments will need to have a pretty strong grasp on their overall theories before fully comprehending their thoughts on totalitarian systems. For those interested in philosophical questions, this need might be a bit time-consuming but not too laborious. But for people with less interest in abstract philosophical issues, this framework can be both daunting and of limited utility.

One mode of understanding totalitarianism (related to the philosophical perspective) that had greater popularity in the 1950s and lost influence over time, but has recently gained some renewed interest, is that of "political religion." This framework starts from the observation that totalitarian systems operate rather differently than normal politics: the fervent zealotry, the worshipful actions toward rulers, the development of various "rituals" and recognition of "martyrs," and the politicizing of all aspects of life (among others) in totalitarianism show substantial, fundamental differences in motivation, vitality, and practices that may not be clear if one only looked at totalitarian systems as governments or as a group of ideas. Contemporary observers, as well as historical researchers, have noted how totalitarian movements often "feel" rather similar to very large cults rather than normal forms of political engagement. Rather than assessing totalitarianism as a political movement, this perspective argues that these systems are better understood as being like religions, even if most are secular (or even explicitly atheistic). Eric Voegelin was one of the first major philosophers to discuss totalitarianism as "political religion" (although he eventually moved away from this framework), but various other philosophers and theorists also used this idea.[17] One major strength of this framework is its attention to the practices and perhaps non-rational elements within totalitarian movements, as it seeks to comprehend the type of passionate activism and dedication one sees within these systems. Among the reasons this framework fell out of favor, however, was that the problem of definition was paramount. Defining "religion" itself can be rather thorny as one tries to be specific, and becomes all the more tricky when attempting to discuss movements as "religious" that often explicitly viewed themselves as against religion (perhaps even replacing religion). In other words, a major criticism was that "political religion" might be using the word "religion" too equivocally, and thus would cause greater confusion than clarity. But, more recently, various scholars, such as Emilio Gentile[18] and A. James Gregor,[19] have brought this idea back to light, and many other scholars are again fleshing out how "political religion" best describes the lived existence of totalitarianism. However, given its previous history, it may take some time to see if this framework gains greater influence.

We should also note the historical method of examining totalitarianism. While the other methods mentioned so far often take a general view of totalitarianism, historical studies tend to focus on more specific regimes, time periods, or individuals/groups. Broader causes and dynamics are often discussed, of course, but the main focus in this framework is providing the "who," "what," "when," and "where" of totalitarian systems, rather than delving as deeply into the "how" and "why." There are some studies that do try to look at totalitarianism broadly, comparing them within historical context.[20] More typically, however, historians usually look at some specific type of totalitarianism (such as Nazism or Marxism-Leninism) rather than as a broader, cross-regime type. As a result, historical studies often concentrate on, among other things, a specific form over time,[21] a specific regime,[22] or perhaps a specific totalitarian leader.[23] Other types of historical investigations will involve comparisons between totalitarian regimes along a specific trait or practice. For instance, there are historical studies of the way totalitarian regimes fight wars against each other,[24] international relations between totalitarian states,[25] or comparing some of the economic reforms in these regimes,[26] among others.

The strengths of the historical framework are rather obvious. These studies provide the actual data and information upon which most other types of investigation are based. Moreover, the focus on detail within historical studies can reveal that superficial similarities between regimes and movements may, in fact, be based on fundamental differences. But its greatest strength is also its largest potential weakness: the attention to specificity can result in losing sight of the "bigger picture" and may incline one to mistakenly view minor differences as essential. In this way, the specificity of the historical framework is a mirror image of the generality of the philosophical framework. One could look at this difference by comparing it with texts in biology: the philosophy framework is rather like a book talking about the fundamental elements of biology (cell structure, genetics, evolution) but provides less guidance about a specific species, while the historical framework is akin to a book that goes in extensive detail about, say, a specific species of frog but gives less insight into life beyond that particular creature.

Finally, we should briefly mention one other type of analysis of totalitarianism that could be called the "partisan" framework. Obviously, most people who research totalitarianism will have rather strong (and negative) personal views on the topic.[27] Such a personal inclination, however, does not necessarily make a text "partisan" in the sense here, as this type of internal motivation is typical for almost any human activity or endeavor (people will usually focus their time on things that are important to them, be it in a positive or negative way). For a work to be "partisan," the examination of totalitarianism is (at least implicitly) aimed at showing that one's political opponents are (or are at potentially) totalitarian in nature. A large portion of these types of works are of little merit. One could look at them as exercises in aspersion and name-calling rather than providing a substantive examination. That said, not all "partisan" texts are worthless. Some can provide interesting additional information and perspectives that one might not find elsewhere,[28] but it is imperative for the reader to always keep in mind the partisan aim in these works.

Researchers use numerous frameworks and methods to understand, or even define, totalitarianism. For someone attempting to get a handle on the concept, however, this variety obviously creates some problems. Trying to provide a summary of these works, much less developing a quick definition that considers this previous research, would be daunting. Moreover, unless one is inclined to study totalitarianism in-depth, trying to read through all these works is rather unworkable. After all, if a person asks, "What is totalitarianism?", it is not terribly useful for someone knowledgeable to respond with, "Here are 25 books – often rather long and heavy on technical language – for you to read. Godspeed, and good luck!" Instead, we might be better served if we examine totalitarianism along a few characteristics, dividing it up (in an analytical sense) into somewhat more manageable parts. If we wanted to understand "democracy," we would probably divide up our study by specifically discussing election practices, the role of rights, and governmental accountability (as just a few possible traits). We should attempt something similar here, dividing our examination of totalitarianism along three different lines:

how totalitarianism "thinks," how totalitarianism organizes itself, and how totalitarianism governs.

Major Characteristics of Totalitarianism

This section will briefly flesh out these three different characteristics, which will also guide the discussion in this rest of this book. But first, it would help to clarify a certain point. When talking about how these characteristics are common in totalitarianism, keep in mind that this indicates how these characteristics provide structural similarities that put different regimes and systems into the same "family." These structural similarities do not mean that the different types of systems are exactly the same, of course. Indeed, many of these systems loathe each other with particular vehemence (as one sees between Nazism and Communism). But these differences should not overshadow some fundamental similarities. A comparison might help, using religion as an example. One way to categorize religions is by the number of deities recognized in them, separating them as monotheistic (believing in one divinity, as in Judaism, Christianity, and Islam), polytheistic (believing in many gods, such as in the Greek and Roman pantheons), and religions that do not have a "god" in the ordinary language sense (such as Buddhism and Taoism). While one could rightly say that Judaism and Islam are in the same "family" of religion, as they are both monotheistic, it is also clear that there are many not-minor differences between them as well. But despite those differences, Judaism and Islam are structurally closer to each other than either would be to, say, the pagan Norse pantheon of gods or to Taoism. The categorizations here are similar. Nazism and Communism have numerous differences between them, but they are structurally more similar to each other than either would be to a typical constitutional democracy, traditional monarchy, or military dictatorship. With that in mind, let's turn to these common traits between totalitarian systems.

First is how totalitarianism "thinks," or ideology. A central commonality in this style of thought is totalism: in other words, that the ideology can explain, at least theoretically, everything regarding human interactions (and perhaps more). In this sense, totalitarian ideology acts as a "master key" to understanding society and history. For most of these ideologies, this "master key" is not itself the political realm. Instead, the "true" driving force of history is something like the conflict between economic classes or between biological races, or perhaps the struggles between religious believers and non-believers. This leads to a second characteristic of totalitarian thinking: deriving from this notion that certain dynamics are "really" the cause for social relations, there are also certain populations that are especially important. To borrow language from the philosopher Georg Wilhelm Friedrich Hegel, these populations are "world-historic": the future direction of human society is dependent upon this population, and the dynamics of society depend substantially upon the fate of this population. Following from the earlier examples, this "world-historic" population could be the working class (or proletariat), the Aryan race, or "true" religious believers, among others. Another key part of totalitarian thinking is its "activist" nature. Whether directly influenced by him or not, these ideologies take a view similar to that of Karl Marx, when he wrote: "The philosophers have only *interpreted* the world, in various ways; the point, however, is to *change* it."[29] These ideologies are not interested in mere observation of the human world, but in shifting the world in a substantially new direction. As such, totalitarian ideologies are inherently revolutionary: they are not interested in reforms of the current form of society, but wish to radically and irrevocably change it, usually through a social revolution. The "world-historic" population has a central role to play in this change. Once this population is dominant, these ideologies usually believe that there will be a new form of society, and, indeed, even a new form of humanity: the creation of a "New Man." This leads to one final commonality to mention here, the negative assessment of the present. Totalitarian ideologies view the present as being inherently wrong in some sense: "oppressive," "irrational," "degenerate," "corrupt," and "impious" would be some of the terms used to describe contemporary society. In this view, these problems are not accidental or temporary, rather they reflect the fundamentally iniquitous structure of the current world. Additionally, those that benefit from this current oppressive system are, by necessity, implacable enemies to the "world-historic" population and the future world itself. As such, the contemporary world must be utterly overturned, the current dominant populations removed (at least from power, and perhaps even from existence), and the "world-historic" population must take control. This could appear to be a fundamental paradox in totalitarian thinking. On the one hand, most totalitarian ideologies view politics as secondary at best, believing something else (economics, biology, theology, or the like) is *really* driving human interaction; on the other hand, in order to revolutionize the world, totalitarian ideology requires the politicization of *every* aspect of human existence. In Chapter 2, we will talk about these factors and more in totalitarian thinking.

If totalitarianism was simply a matter of ideas, then it might be of philosophical interest but practically unimportant. But inherent within totalitarian thinking is the desire for practice: in other words, that the main point of the ideology is to revolutionize the world. To make such a change, organization is necessary. When talking about organization as a characteristic, we are distinguishing between totalitarian organization itself versus totalitarianism as a government. One difficulty with some of the attempts analyzed in the previous section is the level of analysis (for lack of a better phrase). For many of them, they view totalitarianism primarily (or even only) as *governments*. There are good reasons for such a specific focus. First, one can collect a good deal of concrete data on a specific government (with its laws, listed regulations, organizational charts, propaganda materials, and even internal memos or notes between government officials). Second, one might feel more confidence in calling a system "totalitarian" when one can see the actions of the system in government in contrast to the ideas/arguments that serve as the basis for the system. In other words, a system might "sound" non-totalitarian but govern in a totalitarian way, so looking at governments themselves makes categorization easier. Third, one can examine and measure what a government actually *did* in contrast to a social movement or political party that never gained political power, where one has to speculate on what these groups *would have done* had they controlled the government. However, historically, totalitarianism does not simply appear *ex nihilo* from an existing government. Rather, an extended period of ideological and organizational preparation exists before a totalitarian regime gains political power. Social movements arise that demand some type of change (ranging from general reforms to full-out revolution), with organized political groups developing within these movements and shaping these movements. Moreover, various events, experiences, successes, and failures during this movement period can substantially influence how totalitarian governments will model their style of administration later.

In talking about how totalitarianism organizes, we focus on movements and especially on parties. In most cases, totalitarianism develops (and has the greatest success) in periods of significant instability, be it economic, social, political, or even cultural. In these conditions, one usually sees a number of large, mass-based movements arising in a given country. A goodly number of these movements are not, in themselves, totalitarian. They may want some types of reforms, including political reforms (such as giving a larger number of people the right to vote), economic reforms (like advocating for nationalized unemployment insurance), or cultural reforms (for instance, promoting education in local languages), among others. At least initially, totalitarian movements often form as the more extreme "fringes" of these movements. The broader movements often look at these fringes as radical, impractical, and perhaps even rather outlandish, but will usually tolerate the fringe for at least being on the "correct" side (despite their radicalism). In some cases, the totalitarian movement growing within a broader social movement gets greater attention and support. The radicals look more dedicated, less inclined to compromise, and filled with zeal. This situation is especially precarious when the totalitarian movement forms its own political organization – usually a form of a political party. One of the most distinguishing traits of most totalitarian systems is the creation of a "vanguard party." In many ways, the development of this "vanguard" is implicit within totalitarian ideology itself. If there is a "world-historic" population that has a unique role in history, presumably some part of that population will be more "aware" of this role than other members. For many totalitarian ideologies, there is a notion that a large part of the "world-historic" population is blind to its purpose because the awful contemporary world is structured in such a way that this population cannot really "see" what it should do (this inability to see is often called "false consciousness"). But within that population is an "advanced wing" – people dedicated to the ideology who act to advance the "world-historic" population on its way to social revolution. This is the vanguard party: totalitarianism in an organized, political form. The party's role is to mobilize the population and prepare it for social revolution, with the "vanguard" guiding the "world-historic" population along according to the insights of the totalitarian ideology. On a practical level, the major goal of the vanguard party is to take control of the government through whatever means are the most likely to succeed. Sometimes that could mean running candidates for elections, while in other cases it can mean taking power through insurrection, terrorism, and civil war. The vanguard party can also provide an insight into how a particular form of totalitarianism views the role of leadership. Some of these parties will form a leading "committee" to rule the party, while others will emphasize a "leadership principle" that focuses on a particular leader. In some cases, these parties manage to gain control of the government and create a new form of order.

We now come to the third common characteristic: how totalitarianism governs. It is worthwhile to note that totalitarian governments constitute a mere fraction of totalitarian systems. The vast majority of totalitarian movements and parties never manage to gain political control of a country. Some of these parties might gain control of a portion of territory, but lack the ability to establish a recognized state; others may remain on the outskirts of society, never being fully destroyed while also never advancing terribly far; still others are effectively eliminated by the security forces within a state; finally, many just eventually fade out of existence, torn apart by internal disputes or simply never gaining enough popularity to amount to anything. But in some cases – be it from election, insurrection, or war – a totalitarian party does gain and maintain political power. In the popular imagination and memory, the traits we usually associate with totalitarianism relate to its form of government. Among its first acts, totalitarian governments will seek to remove perceived enemies and opponents (by one means or another), as well as engage in massive levels of propaganda. For these leaders, these two actions have central importance. Removing opponents ensures that "enemies of the Revolution" cannot gain any level of power, and propaganda is needed to make sure the country's population begins thinking the "correct" way. As the totalitarian government solidifies its control, it rearranges the political, economic, and social structures of the country, with the vanguard party holding total control over as many spheres of life as possible. Additionally, the government will institute substantial levels of surveillance of the people in the country, which can include encouraging informants, listening in on conversations, reading mail, and other means. In line with the totalistic nature of its ideology, it is not enough for the citizens of a country to acquiesce to the totalitarian regime, or indeed even to generally agree with the regime's actions and aims. The government in these systems, in the end, demand that the citizenry think, perceive, and feel as dictated by the overall ideology of the totalitarian system. To put it another way, when totalitarian systems want total submission, they truly mean *total* submission: submission of the body (following the regulations of the government), submission of the mind ("seeing" reality as the ideology describes it), and submission of the soul (making the totalitarian system and its aims the highest good in one's life, in a manner not dissimilar to how religious believers give themselves over totally to God). Finally, for most totalitarian governments, there will be an inclination toward expansion, be it through subversion of other countries or through explicit warfare. This expansion could be limited to areas viewed as historically "belonging" to the "world-historic" population; expansion might involve invading extended areas to provide "breathing space" for the totalitarian system; and, finally, this expansion might be fundamentally global in nature, with the final aim of transforming the entire world.

There is one other trait that should be mentioned here. Totalitarian governments will often engage in, and maintain, policies that look irrational (or even borderline insane) when viewed from the outside. Historical examples of these policies include regulations on economics that results in widespread famine, as well as expending large amounts of material and labor on exterminating powerless populations during a time of war (when those resources would be better spent on military activities and defense). Indeed, it is rare to find a totalitarian government that does not engage in at least some activities that seem irrational. But here, the central role of totalitarian ideology is important. Even if various totalitarian leaders act opportunistically in many cases, they still believe in the ideology. They truly believe that the ideology explains how reality genuinely works. As a result, these leaders (and other loyal to the totalitarian ideology) will disregard negative reports as "lies" and "enemy propaganda," and will believe that the costs are worth it for a larger and more important goal, or (in some cases) will finally roll back on such policies when the negative results become too overwhelming (and usually, when some new "explanation" arises within the ideology to rationalize what went wrong).

In discussing these three broad characteristics, totalitarianism might appear rather general or abstract. Thus far, we have mostly talked about "totalitarianism" rather generically, rather than "totalitarianism" as concrete instances, such as Stalin's Soviet Union or the Islamic State. If we only talk about general traits and abstract structures, does this really help in understanding totalitarianism as it has actually existed? This is a quite reasonable concern. For this reason, we will specifically focus on the history of totalitarianism after examining these common traits. The intention is that, having provided an analysis of these shared characteristics, the reader can better apply these categorizations to totalitarianism as it has existed in history. Moreover, the hope is that the reader will also have a better sense of how to see possible totalitarianism arising in the future.

Outline of This Book, and Some Additional Notes

The arrangement of the following chapters aims to assist the reader in understanding totalitarianism in its various characteristics. Some of the points mentioned in the last section will come up again, but with much greater level of explanation.

Chapter 2 will discuss totalitarian ideology. As noted earlier, we are looking at the "structure" of the ideologies under consideration, as well as the specific components within any given ideology. This "structure" is the foundation and "skeleton" for general totalitarian ideology, upon which the particular "muscles" and "tendons" of a specific totalitarian ideology is fitted.

For Chapter 3, we turn to totalitarian movements and parties. For reasons based in social/historical development as well as in their ideologies, organization plays a central role for totalitarianism. This chapter will give an overview of how these organizations develop and their common traits (as well as some important differences between them).

It is in Chapter 4 where we will focus specifically on totalitarian governance. We will start by talking about totalitarianism as a "regime type," as a type of government "family." In this sense, democracy, monarchy, military dictatorship, and others would each be a "regime type." This rest of this chapter will flesh out some of the major characteristics in totalitarian government, both in its governing structure as well as in its policies/actions. We will also go over how some differences between totalitarian governments result in substantial differences in how long such a government can maintain power.

We give a brief overview of the history of totalitarianism in Chapter 5. While we will give various historical examples in the previous chapters as a means of clarifying general points of theory and structure, this chapter will provide a partial "timeline" of how totalitarianism has developed in history. We will start by noting some of the major influences and developments from the late eighteenth to the late nineteenth centuries. Then we will turn to what could be called the "Golden Age" of totalitarianism, ranging from late 1917 until around 1953. This is the period when totalitarian regimes held their greatest level of power, and when totalitarianism was often viewed as the "way of the future." We will then go on to talk about totalitarian movements and regimes in the period after the Second World War and conclude with some more recent (especially religion-based) forms of totalitarianism in recent years.

Finally, Chapter 6 will look to the future of totalitarianism. While it would be nice if totalitarianism had no future, it is too early to take such a position. And, indeed, there are reasons to believe that totalitarianism – sometimes in its earlier forms, but also in new variants – is beginning to gain traction again.

In looking through these chapters, the reader might notice a not-insignificant number of endnotes, as well as numerous texts in the chapter bibliographies. It is understandable how the quantity of both could be somewhat off-putting, but fear not. The endnotes will primarily provide citation for references and/or works of use on a topic, or provide some additional context that would be too much of a digression within the chapter itself, so these can be read (or not read) at your leisure. While each chapter will have a "Suggested Readings" section (highlighting the most useful, accessible, or important texts on a topic), the bibliographies are extensive in order to give you a handy list of other sources to examine if some particular topic or idea in the chapter is interesting (and these texts can certainly provide more detailed examination on these things than is possible here).

There is one final thing it would be prudent to note. Totalitarianism is a bane on humanity and highly evil, but we would be mistaken to think of its followers and practitioners as mere villains, psychotics, and/or fools. The spread of these ideologies and regimes was not primarily based on trickery, mass delusion, or even aggravating circumstances in society (such as economic depression). Millions of regular people believed these regimes *were just*, countless intellectuals thought these ideologies *were true reflections of reality*, and most of the main totalitarian leaders truly believed they *were doing the right thing*. If these people were simply criminal or insane, they would have likely caused substantially less destruction. In many ways, this is the most frightening thing about totalitarianism: that thoughtful, well-intentioned, dedicated people could look at these horrors and think they were good and/or acceptable. In understanding totalitarianism, we should aim to not only see how its reasoning and systems work, but also to guard ourselves against falling into similar types of thinking and governance.

Summing Up

- It is important to distinguish between traits that are singular to totalitarianism and traits that may be shared with other types of ideologies/regimes, such as brutality, murder, and surveillance (among others).
- There are many ways to examine totalitarianism (using social scientific methodology, philosophical analysis, historical investigation, and others), each of which provides distinct benefits and limitations.
- In dissecting totalitarianism, we can analytically separate it into its form of *ideology*, its style of *organization/movement*, and its types of *governments/regimes*.

Further Reading

For a good overview of the study of totalitarianism, see Shorten (2015).

For some other overviews on totalitarianism, see Roberts (2020) and Gray (2020).

Notes

1. See various chapters in Geyer and Fitzpatrick (2009).
2. See Gleason (1995).
3. "Operationalization" refers to how social scientists turn some element of life into a numeric variable. Changing something into a number allows for

quantification and measurement. As a simplified example, specifying the political ideology of a member of congress may seem ambiguous, but if a social scientist creates an ideological "spectrum" of bills before congress, then calculating the votes on bills can allow for a numeric measure of ideology. To "operationalize" something, a social scientist will try to give as specific a definition as possible for a trait (or "variable"). As most things consist of multiple traits/variables, social scientists will create "codebooks" that provide their specific definitions so that they (and anyone else, if interested) would be able to "code" (operationalize) the world in the same manner. In this way, social scientists can have greater confidence that the numeric values are valid and that they can be replicated by others. The POLITY dataset is an important example from political science. It provides a scale to indicate the level of democracy that exists in a given country. To create this scale, researchers look at numerous different traits of democracy and make them numeric. In this way, political scientists can use statistical methods to compare various governments over time to examine correlations (and potential causes) in political change. Interested readers can find out more about POLITY at www.systemicpeace.org/polityproject.html.

 4. See Brzezinski and Friedrich (1956).
 5. See Gregor (1979); Gregor (2000).
 6. See Unger (1974).
 7. See Lifton (2017).
 8. See Adorno et al. (2019).
 9. See Arendt (1968).
10. See Arendt (1994).
11. Among others, see Voegelin (1952).
12. See Roberts (2006).
13. Griffin (2007).
14. Shorten (2012).
15. See Sternhell (1994).
16. See Harding (1996).
17. For an overview, see Gray (2014).
18. See Gentile (2006).
19. See Gregor (2012).
20. See Gellately (2007).
21. See Service (2007).
22. See Burleigh (2000)
23. See Kershaw (2000).
24. See Snyder (2010).
25. See Lüthi (2008).
26. See Schivelbusch (2006).
27. The two philosophers previously discussed are good examples. Arendt was a German Jew. After fleeing Germany in 1933, she lived in France for some years until she was briefly interned in 1940 before escaping to the United States in 1941. Voegelin, as a professor in Austria, had written a book denouncing Nazi racial ideology in 1933, arguing that the Nazi racial

ideology was intellectually unsound and pernicious. Immediately following the 1938 annexation of Austria by Germany (called the "Anschluss"), Voegelin fled the country, which was prudent, as officers from the Gestapo (the Nazi Secret Police) came to visit his home within a day of Voegelin's departure.
28. Two examples of this type would be Goldberg (2007) and Stanley (2018).
29. Emphasis in original. Marx (1978): 145.

Bibliography

Adorno, T. W., Else Frenkel-Brunswik, Daniel J. Levinson, and R. Nevitt Sanford. 2019. *The Authoritarian Personality*. London: Verso.

Arendt, Hannah. 1968. *The Origins of Totalitarianism*. New Addition. New York: Harcourt, Inc.

Arendt, Hannah. 1994. *Eichmann in Jerusalem: A Report on the Banality of Evil*. New York: Penguin Books.

Brzezinski, Zbigniew, and Carl F. Friedrich. 1956. *Totalitarian Dictatorship and Autocracy*. Cambridge: Harvard University Press.

Burleigh, Michael. 2000. *The Third Reich: A New History*. New York: Hill and Wang.

Gellately, Robert. 2007. *Lenin, Stalin, and Hitler: The Age of Social Catastrophe*. New York: Vintage Books.

Gentile, Emilio. 2006. *Politics as Religion*. George Staunton, trans. Princeton: Princeton University Press.

Geyer, Michael, and Sheila Fitzpatrick (eds.). 2009. *Beyond Totalitarianism: Stalinism and Nazism Compared*. Cambridge: Cambridge University Press.

Gleason, Abbott. 1995. *Totalitarianism: The Inner History of the Cold War*. Oxford: Oxford University Press.

Goldberg, Jonah. 2007. *Liberal Fascism: The Secret History of the American Left from Mussolini to the Politics of Meaning*. New York: Doubleday.

Gray, Phillip W. 2014. "Vanguards, Sacralisation of Politics, and Totalitarianism: Category-Based Epistemology and Political Religion." *Politics, Religion & Ideology* 15(4): 521–540.

Gray, Phillip W. 2020. *Vanguardism: Ideology and Organization in Totalitarian Politics*. New York: Routledge.

Gregor, A. James. 1979. *Italian Fascism and Developmental Dictatorship*. Princeton: Princeton University Press.

Gregor, A. James. 2000. *The Faces of Janus: Marxism and Fascism in the Twentieth Century*. New Haven: Yale University Press.

Gregor, A. James. 2012. *Totalitarianism and Political Religion: An Intellectual History*. Stanford: Stanford University Press.

Griffin, Roger. 2007. *Modernism and Fascism: The Sense of Beginning under Mussolini and Hitler*. New York: Palgrave Macmillan.

Harding, Neil. 1996. *Leninism*. Durham: Duke University Press.

Kershaw, Ian. 2000. *Hitler: 1936–45: Nemesis*. New York: W.W. Norton & Company.

Lifton, Robert Jay. 2017. *The Nazi Doctors: Medical Killing and the Psychology of Genocide*. Second Edition. New York: Basic Books.

Lüthi, Lorenz M. 2008. *The Sino-Soviet Split: Cold War in the Communist World*. Princeton: Princeton University Press.

Marx, Karl. 1978. "Theses on Feuerbach." In Robert C. Tucker (ed.), *The Marx-Engels Reader*. Second Edition. New York: W. W. Norton & Company, pp. 143–145.

Roberts, David D. 2006. *The Totalitarian Experiment in Twentieth-Century Europe: Understanding the Poverty of Great Politics*. London: Routledge.

Roberts, David D. 2020. *Totalitarianism*. Medford: Polity Press.

Schivelbusch, Wolfgang. 2006. *Three New Deals: Reflections on Roosevelt's America, Mussolini's Italy, and Hitler's Germany, 1933–1939*. New York: Picador.

Service, Robert. 2007. *Comrades: A History of World Communism*. Cambridge: Harvard University Press.

Shorten, Richard. 2012. *Modernism and Totalitarianism: Rethinking the Intellectual Sources of Nazism and Stalinism, 1945 to the Present*. London: Palgrave Macmillan.

Shorten, Richard. 2015. "Rethinking Totalitarian Ideology: Insights from the Anti-Totalitarian Canon." *History of Political Thought* 36(4): 726–761.

Snyder, Timothy. 2010. *Bloodlands: Europe between Hitler and Stalin*. New York: Basic Books.

Stanley, Jason. 2018. *How Fascism Works: The Politics of Us and Them*. New York: Random House.

Sternhell, Zeev. 1994. *The Birth of Fascist Ideology: From Cultural Rebellion to Political Revolution*. David Maisel, trans. Princeton: Princeton University Press.

Unger, Aryeh L. 1974. *The Totalitarian Party: Party and People in Nazi Germany and Soviet Russia*. Cambridge: Cambridge University Press.

Voegelin, Eric. 1952. *The New Science of Politics: An Introduction*. Chicago: University of Chicago Press.

IDEOLOGY
How Totalitarianism Thinks

A central element in understanding totalitarianism is the role of ideology. The difficulty with "ideology" is that it is another one of those words with a number of different connotations, ranging from "a set of ideas/beliefs" to "a closed-minded, unquestioning system of lock-step obedience." While politics can be a fascinating and important area of study, the equivocality of words in its examination does make things trickier, especially for those who are just starting to engage with these topics. For our purposes, "ideology" means a conglomeration of ideas, beliefs, assumptions, and methods of reasoning that generally adhere together in an internally consistent manner. In this sense, it could also be called a "worldview." For ordinary language uses of the term, "ideology" usually has a rather negative connotation, implying that an ideology must be separated in some fundamental ways from reality. Certainly, when Marx and similar writers use "ideology," that is exactly what they mean to convey. But ideology need not have such a subtext. In effect, all people think with an "ideology" (as defined earlier), although these ideologies are not usually terribly rigorous or well-considered – and that is fine! One needs some starting point to assess reality and ideologies (as defined here) are a means by which to start. These ideational structures guide us in determining what is good or evil, what is true or false, and (hopefully) also provide an avenue by which we can critically examine our own ideas and possibly change them.

Obviously, there can be problems with an ideology. It can be wrong on various points of fact, it may not permit much introspection or critique, and, perhaps most damaging, it can expand too far. Theoretically at least, these types of problems could arise in any type

DOI: 10.4324/9781003254232-2

of ideology. Human beings often assume that if something is good in one area, it should therefore be good in all areas, and the more of it the better. Let's give an example of a type of ideology usually presumed to be essentially anti-totalitarian: democracy. Surely, democracy could never be totalitarian, right? And yet, many earlier thinkers (from Plato and Aristotle in ancient Greece to Alexis de Tocqueville in the early 1800s) noted the severe dangers in democratic ideology, with many of these problems sounding rather like totalitarianism. If democracy just means a type of government, and perhaps also describes some norms for how political opponents should interact with each other, then the ideology is properly constrained. But what if one demands a "democratic" form of economy? A "democratic" form of business? A "democratic" form of religious organization? A "democratic" form of family? And keep in mind what these demands would mean: that there is only *one* proper way to organize and think through all aspects of human life. Now it appears that democracy, far from being anti-totalitarian, would (in this form) be highly totalitarian indeed.

Here, we can see our first indication of a trait that makes an ideology totalitarian in nature. One could call this trait a "lack of limiting principle," but perhaps a more concise term would be *totalism*. It is the notion that there is "one true way" for thinking and acting, and that this "one true way" applies, for all intents and purposes, to everything. It may start with political and social systems but tends to expand to other areas of life as well, including things like art, science, and potentially almost anything else. This totalism is why various scholars talk about totalitarian systems as "political religions," insofar as religious systems tend to be totalistic as well. But there are at least two not-minor difference between religion (or many religious traditions, in any case) and totalitarianism. First, while the requirements upon adherents in many religions are totalistic, there is a significant otherworldly aspect to these demands. These responsibilities are from (and aimed toward) a divinity of some type that is fundamentally not of this world. This aspect tends to aim the totalistic elements of religion toward an otherworldly entity, and thus "relieves" the pressure to create a totalistic system on Earth. A second point, related to the first, is that religions traditions with a notion of the end of the world and the final victory of God and the good (the fancy technical term would be "eschatology") usually view the divinity as the one that drives these things, without human knowledge or interaction. While adherents might be able to see the "signs of the times," as it were, human beings lack the ability to bring about the "final judgment."[1] Totalitarian ideologies, on the other hand, tend to lack these two elements (although Islamism, and other religious totalitarian systems, are an obvious exception, as we will discuss in greater detail later). Totalitarian ideologies primarily focus on worldly concerns, and very much believe that humans can – and should – act to bring about an "end of days" or, more specifically, an end of the old (evil, corrupted) world for a "New Society" and the creation of a "New Man."

When talking about ideology of a totalitarian type, we mean its overall *structure* in totalitarian styles of politics and thinking. There is no singular totalitarian ideology. One need only look at the substantial differences in ideology between Communism and Nazism to see that "totalitarian" is more encompassing than a specific set of ideas. Moreover, many of these different totalitarian ideologies loathe each other. One can only imagine just how "pleasant" an interaction in a room between a dedicated Nazi and a fervent Communist (to borrow a phrase popularly attributed to Henry Kissinger, "it's a pity they both can't lose") would be. Rather, it is a structure of ideas and concepts that gives totalitarian ideologies their shape, rather than the specific content in these specific ideologies, even though there will likely be some overlapping elements. Think of it like a building, comparing a family house to a skyscraper. They are two distinct types of structures with a significant amount of variety within each of them. The structures limit and shape the content to a significant extent. A skyscraper is not structured to handle easy access to a white-picket-fenced yard, and a family house lacks the internal ventilation system that would permit dozens of floors. Within these structures, the content can vary quite a bit, be it the wide variation between a quaint country home and a "McMansion" among houses, or the differences in look, use, and height between the Two International Finance Centre in Hong Kong, the Empire State Building in New York City, and the Burj Khalifa in Dubai, for instance. So, too, with totalitarian ideologies. While the content can be quite different, the underlying structure is the generally the same.

In this chapter, we will flesh out what all this means in detail. We will start by focusing on totalism within totalitarian ideologies. Of all the traits in totalitarianism, totalism is the clearest element that distinguishes it from other forms of political thought. We will then turn the role of "History" and populations. The capitalization of "History" is intentional here, as totalitarian ideologies generally have a particular notion of how History operates and believe that understanding the "true" dynamics of History are important for revolutionary change. For most totalitarian ideologies, there are specific populations that play a major role in how political and social changes will play out. Similarly, the main movements and organizations dedicated to creating totalitarian regimes usually view themselves as somehow aligned (or indeed, as the "*avant-garde*") with these populations. Finally, we will be a discussion of what the "New Society" and "New Man" means for these ideologies. Totalitarian thought doesn't aim for reforms – it demands revolution. While often talked about in vague or opaque language, most of these ideologies believe that a "new world" is just around the corner. Once the social revolution succeeds, the world will be substantially and fundamentally different than the world as we have known it. A "better world," and, with it, a new kind of person and humanity will inhabit it.

One other thing should be noted before getting into the structure of totalitarian ideology. A consistent point made by numerous scholars[2] is that totalitarianism is a specifically *modern* phenomenon, which means the period after the Renaissance and especially from about the 1700s into the present. That totalitarianism is modern does not mean it is completely unrelated to earlier forms of movements. Indeed, totalitarian ideology (at least) could be viewed as a type of millenarianism,[3] of which there has been no shortage in the past,[4] and could also be seen as part of a style of thinking that Eric Voegelin identified as "Gnostic" in nature.[5] All that said, there are traits of modernity – certain forms of Enlightenment thinking, the increased secularization of Western society, the Industrial Revolution and exponential technological growth, and the rise of mass politics, among others – that are tightly connected to most forms of totalitarianism and are missing in earlier periods. So, if it looks like the focus is solely on the last few centuries, that is fully intentional.

Totalism

As the name "totalitarian" implies, there is a strong element of totalism within these ideologies. "Totalism" means that the ideology – at least in theory – touches on every aspect of human life. There is nothing "outside" of the totalitarian ideology. While, obviously, these ideas will have a great deal to say regarding social interactions, political life, and similar things, they are also the measure for familial life, hobbies, the "correct" view of art, and even the sciences. One can properly say that, for totalitarian systems, "everything in the ideology, nothing outside the ideology, nothing against the ideology" (to paraphrase an infamous line from Mussolini on the State). Various scholars use a similar notion when they refer to the "monist" structure of totalitarian ideology,[6] meaning that this one central idea (or rather, constellation of ideas, assumptions, and beliefs) dictates the manner in which all human existence is perceived. Usually, this monistic totalism is based on some notion of an underlying "dynamic" or group of processes that "really" drive human society. If one understands this dynamic – the "science" of it, as it were – a person could truly know not only the actual motors of contemporary society, but also the direction in which humanity will go. The ideology acts like a "key" from which you can understand everything else. If one considers the language of some of the more "mainstreamed" forms of totalitarian thinking that one sees today (discussed more in Chapter 6), terms like "woke" or "red-pilled" reflect this idea. Once your "eyes are opened" to the "real" foundations of human interaction, then everything else follows. This monist, totalistic idea becomes the "master science," where a person (theoretically, at least) could understand all human life based upon it.

Communist ideology provides a good example. The basis for most Communist thought (at least as derived from Marxism and Leninism) is that economics shapes human society (and, specifically, who controls the "means and modes of production"). As a broad statement, there are many people – including staunch anticommunists – who would generally agree with that idea: that how things are made, and who controls that flow of creation, substantially influences what types of morals, customs, and rules exist in a society. But the totalitarian Communist ideology takes this idea much further: that these economic structures not only influence political systems or laws (for instance), but also fundamentally *determine* them, as well as determine daily interaction, what we deeply believe, what art we consider better or worse, the socially viewed notion of the "proper" family, how we talk, how we engage in science (determining what counts as evidence, what counts as an experiment), and even how we perceive reality and *think*. What this could mean in practice (looking to the Soviet Union for various examples) would include domination of the economy by the State, "revolutionary" forms of law/justice (where guilt is often based on one's economic class, rather than anything a person actually did), encouraging children to act as informants against their parents, enforcing the use of euphemisms ("liquidating" rather than "executing"), and enforcing a "class-conscious" form of biology among geneticists (as seen with Lysenkoism).[7] Starting from an idea that, broadly stated, seems like something that might be correct or at least have some truth to it, the totalitarian takes that idea to cover anything and everything, with some rather severe results.

In some cases, the ideas are quite explicit, even if their interpretation undergoes change. For instance, the role of the "mass line" as well as the constant referencing of "Mao Tse-Tung Thought"[8] during the Cultural Revolution (1966–1976) made the ideology inescapable for people in China. In other cases, the ideas are pushed through organizations rather than through some central text and depend more upon an attempt to follow the desires of a particular leader. A good example of this form would be Nazi Germany. A major focus of the regime was ensuring *Gleichschaltung* (roughly translated as "coordination") so that all groups (from major institutions to even minor hobbyist associations) would maintain the "proper" allegiance to Nazi ideology. However, despite references to *Mein Kampf*[9] and various speeches, there was no singular text or group of texts that could provide ideological guidance[10] (in contrast to Communist societies, where the works of Marx – and frequently, of Lenin – served that role, at minimum). Developments in Nazi ideology and practice instead derived from "working towards the Führer," where members acted in "anticipation of Hitler's presumed wishes and intentions as 'guidelines for action' in the certainty of approval and confirmation for actions that accorded with those wishes and intentions."[11] Whether embodied in a groups of texts, an organization, and/or a specific person, it is the totalistic "idea" (or perhaps better considered as a constellation of ideas) that drives and directs changes. When we turn to totalitarian regimes in Chapter 4, we will see how these types of authorities intermix with each other when a totalitarian government is in power.

The all-embracing nature of these worldviews is a central trait that distinguishes totalitarian ideologies from other types of political/philosophical frameworks. This is important to note, as both totalitarian ideologies and non-totalitarian systems can focus on similar populations, ideas, and issues. Someone focused on economic redistribution is not a communist, a person concerned with maintaining national customs is not a fascist, and even someone who researches possible genetic group-level differences between races is not a Nazi. In each of these cases, the ideas of these people are limited to certain spheres or policy areas, where large swaths of human life would be untouched by their ideas (or touched on at most in a reductive and truistic sense[12]). That is not the case for totalitarian ideologies. All aspects of life can – and *should*, in the totalitarian's view – be explained by the ideology. In ordinary language, this type of distinction often gets obscured. Once again, this is where the lack of a limiting principle is a big trait in totalitarian ideologies. As a general rule of thumb, if a political/social ideology appears to expand to everything – and where there does not seem to be any internal restraint in the ideology itself against this type of spread – it is exhibiting a tendency (at least) toward totalitarian ideology.

What totalism means in practice depends significantly upon the specific ideology of a totalitarian system itself. While all of them share a similar "structure" in terms of their totalistic ideas, there are obviously major differences in content between them. Similarly, some totalitarian systems have undergone extensive amounts of work fleshing out their ideologies, while others (either because of the content itself, or resulting from a lack of time) are perhaps more impressionistic in nature. The Communist regimes of the Soviet Union and the People's Republic of China give the best example of totalism getting comparative free reign in practice. After its victory in the Russian Civil War (1917–1923), the Communist Party had effectively eliminated internal opponents, including both the supporters of the Tsarist government and the "White Army," but also former allies, such as the Social-Revolutionaries and (to an extent) the Mensheviks. Similarly, the Chinese Communist Party had exterminated most opponents by the end of the Chinese Civil War in 1949. This "clearing the deck" of possible contenders for power, be they dedicated opponents or merely groups/parties that had some disagreements with the Communists, allowed the

Communists to generally govern as they saw fit, as there were no real internal (political) obstacles in their path. Both of these regimes had decades to flesh out totalism in practice, with results we will discuss more in Chapters 4 and 5.

In contrast, the Italian Fascists and German Nazis had greater limits on fulfilling their totalistic desires in two ways. The first constraint was what Nazis referred to as the "path of legality." Rather than gaining power through insurrection and civil war (as was the case for the Communists in Russia and China), the Fascists and Nazis (in their own ways) attempted to at least appear to act in partially legal ways to gain power, and often lacked the ability to eliminate other contenders for power at the start of their respect governments. For instance, Mussolini's Fascist Party in Italy took power in flamboyant fashion with its "March on Rome" in 1922, but two things stand out. First, while the Fascists were considering a full-on insurrection against the Italian government, it did not, in the end, become necessary. Italy's King Victor Emmanuel III appointed Mussolini as prime minister instead. This is important insofar as the Fascists (and Mussolini in particular) gained power through the previous regime. Unlike the Communists, they did not make a "clean sweep" of opponents on their way to power. Second, Mussolini and the Fascist Party initially still had limits upon them from the earlier system, only becoming bolder after two years (when they changed the election laws), and only being capable of explicitly declaring a dictatorship in 1928. As other important political actors (such as the Italian monarchy, the Roman Catholic Church, and others) remained in Italy, the Fascists were stymied from fully developing their system. Even when reconstructed in the "Republic of Salò" (1943–1945), the Fascists were effectively running a mere client state for Nazi Germany. As for the Nazis themselves, Hitler strategized the "path of legality" after the failed "Beer Hall Putsch" in Munich (1923), and after his own short stint in jail (1924). It was not until the early 1930s that the Nazis gained significant power and Hitler himself gained the role of chancellor (1933). As a result, it took a few years for the Nazi regime to fully consolidate its power, as potential opponents still existed. While the "path of legality" aided these ideologies by preventing civil war from breaking out, it also meant that neither the Fascists nor the Nazis could start from a "blank slate." In both cases, the Fascist and Nazi parties had to spend their first years working with institutions and elites that the Communists had managed to eliminate in their own countries.

The second constraint was time. Even including the earlier parts of their regimes, the Fascist and Nazi ideologies only ruled over their countries for 21 years and 12 years, respectively. Unlike the Soviet regime (lasting about 70 years, depending upon one's chosen start date) and the PRC (still going after 73 years), the Fascists and Nazis lacked the time to flesh out their totalism to the fullest – although seeing the damage the Nazis managed to do during their limited time in power, one can only imagine what horrors would have come from a longer lifespan. Another totalitarian ideology limited by time was the Islamic State. While it still exists, somewhat, at the time of this writing (mid-2022), it is mere shadow of its previous strength. Like the Communists, the Islamic State managed to gain control through civil war and insurrection; but unlike in Russia and China, the Islamists faced ongoing pressure not only from local populations, but also from the military activities of the United States, the Russian Federation, and various other national militaries.

We should mention one other example here, insofar as it is a rather strange but notable one: North Korea (although, to an extent, we could also possibly use the historical example of Albania under Enver Hoxha as well). North Korea is one of the longest-lasting totalitarian regimes, but not totalitarian ideologies. To be more specific, North Korea's ideology was initially a form of Stalinist Communism, but over time it modified itself to what the regime called the "*juche*" ideology,[13] taking on a more nationalistic form of totalism. According to a recent study, it now appears that the North Korean ideology is shifting toward a more racialist form of totalism.[14] On its face, these changes would seem bizarre. The ruling party (and ruling family) remains the same, and yet the totalistic ideology shows major changes. But in another sense, this is not so confusing. As mentioned earlier, totalitarian ideologies share a similar "structure" for their ideas. That being the case, shifting from one type of totalistic ideology (focused on class conflict) to another type of totalism (based on nation or race) is simpler than changing to something structurally different (like constitutional democracy, monarchy, or others).

The ideology of totalitarianism seeks control of all aspects of life. This is its "totalism" in a nutshell. We have already mentioned how traditional religions can also be totalistic, but in ways that are not

totalitarian. We can also consider other types of ideas that are totalistic that may not necessarily totalitarian, such as the notion that
science covers everything (in other words, that all things – including
human minds and interactions –can be reduced in the end to material
causes). Are there other traits to totalitarianism that would distinguish
it from these other types of totalism? Indeed, there are. Totalitarian
ideology usually entails a specific type of methodology in its thinking, focused on population groups, history, and its notions of what
"really" causes societies to move and change. It is to these aspects we
turn next.

History, the Dynamics of Society, and Populations

Before starting this section, a head's-up for the reader. This section is going to be rather heavy on abstract – and to an extent,
obscure – philosophical reasoning. Philosophy itself can often be a
bit tricky to grasp, and the philosophies we'll be talking about here
are considered pretty rough, even among professional philosophers,
theorists, and intellectual historians. In a sense, one might say that
it is almost fitting that to understand totalitarianism would require
the pain of delving into borderline incomprehensible philosophical
systems, but we'll leave such musing to the side. In other words,
if you find that it takes a few read-throughs to get a handle on the
concepts and styles of thinking in this section, don't worry. This
does not necessarily indicate a problem with you, as this material is
indeed quite complicated and murky.

One thing that remains pretty typical for totalitarian ideologies is
the focus on specific populations. There are strict divisions within
these forms of thought between those groups that are considered
good and "world-historic" versus those that are evil and embody
the current, corrupt age. "World-historic," a phrase derived from
the German philosopher G. W. F. Hegel (1770–1831), whose work
influenced numerous totalitarian ideologies and thinkers (including
Karl Marx), means a population that is "in sync" with "History."
Hegel's work can be a bit dense, to put it mildly, so let's unpack some
of these ideas. In this style of thinking, be it Hegel's or that of later
totalitarian ideologies, there is a substantial difference between "history" and "History." The contingent and accidental elements of the
passage of time would be "history" (in the lowercase). These would

be the types of events and facts that one might see in a typical history book or chronicle, such as "Levi P. Morton was the vice president of the United States in 1891." For most of these thinkers, this type of history can provide data and may be of some interest but lacks greater meaning or importance. On the other hand, "History" (in the upper-case) is vitally important. This type of History is not accidental, but instead reflects the fundamental dynamics of (at least) human existence. This History is the "engine," as it were, of how humanity develops, evolves, and changes. In Hegel's philosophy (at least in some interpretations),[15] the ongoing drive for "Spirit" or "Mind" (*Geist* in German) to its full actualization in itself – which would also result in full human liberty – is what moves History. All of the truly major and important changes throughout the development of the world are driven by this overarching end of *Geist*'s actualization.

What this means is probably a bit murky. There are various ways scholars and others have interpreted *Geist*. Some view it as a divine thing working through History to become fully God (in some sense or another); others interpret *Geist* as the "full actualization" of humanity, meaning that human beings would reach its full perfection in its faculties, social arrangements, and freedom; and still others see *Geist* as a type of natural "order" coming to its final conclusion. But whatever this *Geist* is, it acts as the dynamic that moves humanity along in a determinate, specific "direction," reflective of the "progress" of History. While also deriving from an earlier German philosopher (Immanuel Kant), among others, if you hear people unironically say that they are (or desire to be) on the "Right Side of History," they are mouthing Hegelian notions of "progress," even if they don't realize it. This type of History often works without the knowledge or intention of those involved. Rather, History works "through" certain types of individuals and populations. Hegel's philosophy is usually considered a form of idealism (focused on the centrality of ideas, thought, and the nonmaterial), but its general structure would be used by a variety of different totalitarian ideologies, whether "idealist," "materialist," or something else.

So, in turning to totalitarian ideology, what are these fundamental dynamics of History? This is where the various types of totalitarian ideologies differ. For Communists (and Marxists of various kinds), the main dynamic is economic. Changes in technology are key, but the ownership of the "means of production" (the most essential economic technology of a given time) is of greater social (and Historical) importance. The changes in ownership of the "means of production" cause broader changes in all human interaction, as seen in the shift from slavery-based economies to feudalism to capitalism: the shift of ownership from warlords (where exploited humans were also mere property) to ownership by hereditary aristocracy (where the exploited humans were serfs, working on land owned by the aristocrats) to ownership by capitalists (where the exploited humans are workers, working in factories owned by the capitalist class). With each of these differences of ownership reflecting technological changes (agricultural, industrial, and the like), widespread social changes also occur in terms of what types of political systems are considered legitimate, what types of questions are "settled" regarding reality, and what types of morals dominate, such as the shifts from the martial spirit of the warlord days to the intricate rules of the nobility to the dull but studious *mores* of the bourgeoisie. For Nazis and similar racialist views, the main dynamic is biological. The ongoing process of biological evolution at the group level (usually viewed as by race and/or ethnicity) creates a dynamic of inherent group conflict, rather like the process of "survival of the fittest" within and between other species. These racial/ethnic groups seek greater "survivability" through maintaining group cohesion against other groups, including genetic cohesion. In this racialist view, the dynamic of History reveals itself in both the rise of more "pure," "superior" types of races, but also in "degeneration" caused by permitting "dysgenic" members of the race/ethnicity to live and reproduce with other ("lower") races/ethnicities. Communist and Nazi (or, if you prefer, economically focused and biologically focused) ideologies, despite their obvious differences on the dynamics of History, do share an underlying assumption that History is materialistic. In other words, that the fundamental "engine" of History is something physical, with ideas often reflecting (or even caused by) these material bases. This does not mean that economically or biologically focused ideologies think ideas are irrelevant – far from it. Rather, these ideologies believe that at the most fundamental and basic level ideas primarily derive from material circumstances – that certain types of worker solidarity can only arise in a society with a highly developed division of labor and an advanced level of industrialization (for the Communists), or that certain types of moral or cultural norms can only arise "bio-culturally" within specific genetic populations (for Nazis). In terms of priority and importance, it is these material causes that "drive" History. When we discuss some ecologically focused totalitarian ideologies, we will see this material-ism again. Totalitarian forms of nationalism, on the other hand, vary rather significantly from this materialist notion type of History. For them, ideas and culture (specifically national culture, *mores*, language, customs, and the like) are a key part of Historical dynamics. Ethnic-ity can also play a role, but, oftentimes, totalitarian nationalism fix-ates more on the notion of persons/populations "having the feel" of the nation rather than being focused on genetic similarities. In this sense, someone with a mixed racial background who fully embodied the cultural elements of the nation would be more acceptable than someone born and raised in the country who subscribed to "foreign" or "cosmopolitan" mentalities. Fascist Italy – at least before its alli-ance with Nazi Germany began to have some influence – is a good example. The Fascist Party itself initially had Jewish members, and the primary internal enemies in the Fascist worldview were "inter-nationalist proletarians" (Italians who aligned with Marxism and the Soviet Union) and "cosmopolitan bourgeoisie" (Italians focused on international finances to the detriment of Italy itself).[16] In this sense, they share similarities to Hegel's own idealism and some types of religion. Indeed, some of the religiously focused ideologies will be similar to the totalitarian nationalists.

Still with me? Excellent. I salute your endurance.

It might seem as if human beings – individually or as groups – are rather irrelevant in this form of History. After all, if these processes move on their own, wouldn't humans just be spectators to it all? This is where we now turn to the "world-historic" population. Earlier, we noted how Hegel viewed *Geist* as working "through" popula-tions for History's movements. The totalitarian ideologies share this general notion, but ditch *Geist* for what are viewed as more con-crete (and often "scientific") dynamics as moving History, such as economics or biology. In this view, certain populations arise within History to move humanity along its path. In most instances, this "world-historic" group is a distinct mass population, be it an eco-nomic class (the proletariat of Communist fixation), a nation (such as Italy for the Fascists), a race (the "Aryan race" for Nazism), or others. Usually, these ideologies will also note past populations that held "world-historic" importance. For instance, Communists would point to the bourgeoisie of France in the late 1700s as being "world-historic" in moving society from feudalism to capitalism, but that these past "world-historic" populations had served their "function" and had either long ceased to exist or (more unpleasantly) continued to perpetuate the contemporary and "obsolete" form of society. While these past groups are of theoretical interest to the totalitarians, their main focus is on the contemporary "world-historic" population, often viewed as the ultimate one: the population that will bring about the final culmination and conclusion of History as we know it. The three types mentioned previously (proletariat, nation, and Aryan race) would be key examples. For the Communists, the victory of the working class would bring about the final end of the dynamic of History. The "classless society" would arise and the conflict that drove History since its beginnings would cease, with a full, "true" humanity arising. Moreover, this final stage of History was inevitable in the Communist worldview. The proletariat bringing about the classless society was as certain and necessary as the laws of gravity. The Nazis were a bit different. They, too, saw the rise of the Aryan race as bringing about a new humanity, but because of their view of how the dynamics of History work, they also believed it was fully possible that the "world-historic" society might fail in its mission, leading to the utter degeneration of humanity. Many of the Fascists they tended to view History as a set of "cycles." While there was not a clear "end," like with the Communists, they did believe that the "ups" and "downs" of the cycle could be known (so, in the Italian case, that a "New Renaissance" was on the horizon). While, again, the structure of totalitarian ideologies are similar, the differences in content can lead to some major differences in what conclusions these ideologies draw.

Totalitarian ideologies – and later, their movements and regimes – will often present themselves as advocating for the "true" interests of this "world-historic" population, even if that population itself may not "realize" it. The totalitarian ideology explicates the "real" aims, interests, and future for the special population in itself, rather than what any specific individual member of that population may actually want. To use the Communist example, the totalitarian ideology presents the "real" aims of the working class as seeking the overthrow of the capitalist system and the establishment of a classless society, even if the concrete desires of actual individual (even the majority of) workers are rather more simple and mundane (like higher pay or better working conditions). But wouldn't the "world-historic" population already know its own interests? Why would it need a totalitarian ideology to "realize" its interests? The problem, in the view of these ideologies, is that a large portion (indeed, perhaps most) of the "world-historic" population has been miseducated, lives under illusions, and has been constrained in its thinking due to the overwhelming influence of the current, "corrupt" form of society. A useful phrase for this view is "false consciousness," a term coming from Marxian ideology but equally useful for other types of totalitarian ideology. "False consciousness" not only explains why the "true interests" of a population don't seem to match what members of these populations say that they want, but also provides a foundation for the primary form of totalitarian political organization that totalitarian movements will use: the "vanguard party" (which we will discuss in great detail in Chapter 3).

Many of these thinkers will also claim that they are not speaking about morals, but are instead being brutally scientific in their thinking.[17] That may seem a little odd from an outside perspective, as the language of totalitarians uses a plethora of moralistic language, especially when talking about the "unjust" nature of the current system and/or the evil of their opponents ("parasites," "bloodsuckers," and "vermin" tend to be popular terms). But, in the minds of totalitarian ideologues, they have discovered certain laws, dynamics, or truths that make the end result they desire a necessary event. Or, to speak anachronistically, they could say that their descriptions of social revolution are the same as scientists talking about the absorption of the Earth by the Sun in a few billion years; it is not that the scientists are saying it *ought* to happen or that it would be *morally better* if it happened, but rather that it is just a statement about a *necessary cause and effect*. As is often the case, the origins of this focus are in the discussions within Marxism, and most clearly fleshed out in *Socialism: Utopian and Scientific* by Marx's regular co-author, Frederick Engels.[18] One of the Marxists' major criticisms of earlier socialist thinkers and activists was that these types were "utopian." The early socialists were arguing what would be morally better to do and attempting to persuade others of the justness of their views. For Marxists (and many other totalitarians), this was pie-in-the-sky optimism. Those with power would not be convinced to lose their position based on moral persuasion. But of even greater importance to this view is that moral persuasion is not how changes occur in society. In practice, moral discourses and norms are "pushed along" by more foundational, fundamental dynamics. To borrow the language of some Marxists, things like law and morality are "superstructure," while economic relations and technology are "structure." Laws and morality "rest upon" and are shaped by the foundations of economic relations. For the Marxists (and for other totalitarians that share this style of thinking), it is this "scientific" understanding of true History that makes their claims about the social revolution leading to a "classless society" and the like non-utopian (even if their "New Society" sounds awfully utopian). Earlier socialists were like an insane man shouting on a street corner about a better world, while the Marxian socialists were like a scientist tracing the paths of planets or explaining chemical reactions.

Naturally, there is some duplicitous framing going on as well. Specific terms may be used that can have both moralistic and "scientific" (or at least analytic) components. Consider more contemporary examples of someone discussing LGBTQ+ populations and referring to them as "deviants," or someone referring to conservative Western political parties as "white supremacist." In both cases, the words have dual implications, one being moralistic and negative ("deviant" as similar to "degenerate," "white supremacist" as similar to "bigot" or "Nazi"), and another being at least potentially analytic and neutral ("deviant" as a statistical term referring to populations/datapoints outside the central "cluster" of instances; "white supremacist" as referring to a technical term in various types of critical theory-style analysis). In some cases, the speaker may, indeed, simply be speaking analytically without any intended negative connotation. But in other cases, particularly when speaking to non-specialist audiences, playing off of both meanings is intentional. When totalitarians describe their views of "scientific" or "non-moral," they are often playing this type of two-faced game. They can take in the benefits of stirring moralistic rhetoric while simultaneously claiming to be merely looking at things in a "scientific" manner.

So far, we have mostly provided examples from totalitarian ideologies that base themselves on something recognizably materialist (like economics or biology) or cultural (like nations). There are cases, however, where an ideology primarily bases itself on something non-human, rather than on a mass population. The most obvious examples are totalitarian ideologies that base themselves on some notion of religion/divinity and others based upon radical environmentalism.[19] As these two types of ideology have gained greater prominence in recent decades, we will finish this section by giving them a bit more attention.

Religious totalitarian ideologies present some complexities that are generally lacking in the typical, historical versions of totalitarianism. Most contemporary religions are totalistic, at least in their theologies (even if not always in practice). There is no sphere of life outside the concern and interest of God (or the Divine order, however conceptualized). This totalism contrasts with some ancient forms of religion, where the divinities worshipped might only care about certain aspects of life, be generally indifferent to human activities, or indeed might seem rather capricious in terms of what mattered and what did not (as one can see in the various myths and stories of pagan Greece and Rome, for instance). The religions today, however, also tend to emphasize the otherworldly nature of this totalism. Barring some major eschatological event that is solely in God's control, like the Last Judgment in Christianity, the rule of the divine is not "of" this world. Certainly, religious believers will attempt to influence government policies based upon their own theologies and practices, but there is as wide a gulf between religiously informed policy preferences and theocratic totalitarianism as there is between union-focused social democracy and Stalinist totalitarianism. To use Voegelin's language, mentioned in Chapter 1, contemporary religions are not "immanentized" in the sense of bringing "heaven on Earth" by seeking to bring God's rule directly into the world via some party, church, or other organization.

This distinction, however, becomes rather more challenging when considering the primary example of religious totalitarianism in the current era, political Islamism or jihadism.[20] Unlike Christianity, Islam does not have a similar strict distinction between "Caesar" and "God" (between the religious and the political realms).[21] Rather, the law of God is supposed to reign supreme over a state in the *dar al Islam*, although forced conversion is not considered an acceptable part of this system. What distinguishes jihadist totalitarianism (of the type seen in the ideologies of Al Qaeda or the Islamic State) from the general Islamic religion as it interacts with politics is its totalistic nature. Certainly, there are no shortage of religious laws within an Islamic country (such as Saudi Arabia or Qatar, for instance), but Islamist totalitarianism is more all-encompassing. Beyond the law, the entire culture (and each individual within it) must be fully submissive to the rule of God. One should keep in mind that Islamism – just like totalitarianism in general – is a modern occurrence. Indeed, it only really started to develop in the early part of the twentieth century, and gets its best theoretical exposition in the Sayyid Qutb's works. It should also be noted that, for Islamist totalitarian ideology, there are few to no "truly" Islamic countries in the world, but instead there exists a plethora of "pagan" societies ("*jahiliyyah*") dominated by corrupt monarchs, petty dictators, or worse. As Qutb (1906–1966, a leading Islamist thinker) puts it, "all societies existing in the world today are *jahili*".[22] While Islamist totalitarian ideology exists in numerous types of groups (be it Al Qaeda, the Abu Sayyaf Group, Boko Haram, or others), it has thus far only shown itself as a regime – be it so temporarily – in the Islamic State of 2013 to approximately 2017.

Finally, let's consider ecological totalitarian ideology. This type is comparatively recent, so we can only present some rather broad outlines. There are ideologies and perhaps some groups in extreme environmentalism that we could identify as totalitarian, but, thus far, none of them are influential enough to present a clear challenge to a political system. One of the difficulties in thinking through eco-totalitarianism is the manner in which it "blurs" with other forms of environmentalism, which is likely a reflection of the comparatively recent nature of this new form of environmental concern.[23] We can, however, point to various groups and individuals that provide at least a framework for the underlying ideologies. These can include animal-focused groups like the Animal Liberation Front (ALF), broader eco-terror groups like the Earth Liberation Front (ELF), some earlier groups such as Earth First! (EF!), and finally individuals such as Theodore Kaczynski (popularly known as the "Unabomber").[24] The linking element between the disparate forms of eco-totalitarianism is the central focus on the "planet," "nature," or some similar ecologically focused notion. The critiques can vary, but often the ideologies focus on society being too "human-centric," the debilitating and self-perpetuating nature of modern technology, and sometimes more mystical notions. These ideologies are pretty niche at the moment, but they may become more daunting threats in the future (discussed more in Chapter 6).

So far, we have looked at how totalitarian ideologies think about reality and how they tend to frame their critiques of contemporary societies. But most of them will also paint, in rather broad strokes, a vision of a brighter, better tomorrow: the "land of milk and honey," as it were, once the social revolution succeeds. So, what does this "New Society" look like in the minds of totalitarian ideologies?

The "End" of History: New Society, New Man

For most totalitarian ideologies, there is a "final end" (or at least a substantive change in kind rather than degree) that comes into view, where the dynamics that created the negative world of the present are swept away to be replaced with a glorious, better world. These types of ideologies tend to view History as like a story, with a beginning, a middle, and an end. The beginning usually involves a simpler time (like a "prehistory" of humanity, or at least human society), until some change occurs that triggers the dynamics of "History" to start. This change could be the creation of private property, the increased intermixing of tribal groups, or some other change. This change is usually viewed as negative, but also as a change that is necessary to advance humanity toward its final end.[25] The middle of the story is most of recorded history, with the rise and fall of civilizations and cultures, but with this history being driven by the underlying dynamics of History itself. As a result, many of the major events of regular "history" may be minor in a "true" understanding of History. Many totalitarian thinkers view themselves as being at the latter part of the middle of the story on the cusp of the conclusion of the narrative. A major aim of totalitarian thought is to bring about the end of the story. With the "world-historic" population taking down the corrupt present system through social revolution, we reach the "end of History" (or, in other cases, the next, "higher" stage of humanity). The types of typical evils in the present will be washed away, and the "true" story of humanity – a humanity freed from oppression, corruption, and evils – can finally begin. Or, so the totalitarian ideologies believe, in any case.

One thing that most totalitarian thinkers will emphasize is that their focus on the "end" of History is not utopian, which at first seems a bit contradictory. Isn't the focus on a "perfect" future the epitome of utopian thinking? This seems quirky, but fits into the earlier discussion on totalitarian thinkers proclaiming that they are not "utopians," but are instead thinking "scientifically." For these types of thinkers, there is a substantial difference between ideologies that argue that something *should* exist that we should aim to create (which would be "idealist" and "utopian") and ideologies that examine what *will* exist according to the ironclad dynamics of History regardless of human will (which would be "scientific" and "realistic"). As such, totalitarian ideologues truly believe they are not being "utopian" even if their "scientific" view of the future after the social revolution sounds as unrealistic as pigs flying or turning the oceans into lemonade.

So far, we have mostly focused on ideas (and the populations associated with them). But totalitarianism is not merely an exercise in theorizing, like one might see with an eccentric group of mathematicians attempting to describe all human life through some extended interpretation of number theory. The point of these ideas is to change the world, and to change it radically. Rather implicit in the "final end" of history is the ascension of a new type of humanity, which in earlier totalitarian ideologies was usually referred to as the creation of the "New Man": the better world would be populated by a better humanity than the one we see in the present. The characteristics of this "New Man" and "New Society" depend pretty heavily upon the specific totalitarian ideology. One consistency between all of them, however, is that the types of corruptions and evils of the earlier system will vanish once the "world-historic" population wins and the evil "Enemy" population "disappears" (by one means or another) and issues like class oppression or racial-mixing (or whatever else) will cease to exist. The "New Society" will be thriving, vital, and "free." "Freedom" here means something rather different from its usual sense. To be "free" often entails to be fully what people are supposed to be – to be fully "authentic" or the like. It often entails being freed from bad habits, incorrect styles of thinking, and oppressive societal structures that impel people toward marginalization or other evils. One sees this as early as the French Revolution, where the major changes of that time "engendered a surge of near millenarian hopes for a world transformed, in which a 'new man' might take control of his destiny and forge a society based on reason, equality, and universal brotherhood."[26]

Perhaps one of the most glaring things in totalitarian thought is the absence of a clear idea about what this "New Society" (and the "New Man" who populates it) would look like. Certainly, there is no shortage of almost sloganeering-like phrases – the "classless society," the "racially superior/pure society," a "New Renaissance," or the like – but rather less concrete details. "Equality," "reason," "purity," and the like all sound very nice, but what would it mean in practice? If the social revolution succeeds, what types of decision-making bodies will exist (as the contemporary state "withers away")? If the "patriarchal" family is destroyed, how are children reared and raised in the "New Society?" These and numerous other types of "nuts-and-bolts" questions come up when hearing about the "New Society," and, generally, there are few answers provided by totalitarian ideologies. We can point to two major reasons for this paucity of exposition. The first reason comes from most totalitarian thinkers themselves. Based on their notion of History, they argue that clear details on the "New Society" is, at best, fragmentary and partial. As these thinkers are still operating within the "middle" part of the story, they can only "see" the broad strokes of the conclusion "through a glass darkly," as it were. As thinkers born, raised, and living in a class-based society or a racially mixed country, they argue that their own minds are still shaped by the dynamics that currently exist. A new world without class struggle or racial heterogeneity is so foreign that it is beyond the thinkers' ability to flesh out. It would be rather like asking someone born and raised in the middle of a desert to describe how someone should pilot a ship on an ocean. For these thinkers, spending too much time speculating about the "New Society" in detail would run the danger of becoming "utopian" in nature. The second reason is less complimentary to the totalitarian thinkers. Specifics about the "New Society" would give some measures for success and some standards to which the totalitarian ideology could be held accountable. If the end of class struggle would result in a better quality of life for all workers, or if removing racial heterogeneity would produce a stronger/smarter/more attractive racial population, the population of a country will start to ask when these excellent outcomes will finally arrive. As we will note in our discussion of totalitarian regimes in Chapter 4, the problem of standards arises pretty frequently, as populations in totalitarian societies do start to wonder when all of these good things will finally come into existence. Additionally, at least for some totalitarian thinkers, they may be somewhat disinclined to talk too specifically about the "New Society" because of what that discussion might imply about other groups. What, practically, does it mean to say that the bourgeoisie or racial "inferiors" will "disappear"? Presumably, they are not going to "fade away" willingly, and certainly it would raise some unpleasant questions regarding what would happen to these people. In a strong sense, the details on the "New Society" could present a disconcertingly clear view of the underlying logic of extermination needed to create the "New Man."

Conclusion

Ideas, on their own, are immobile. An idea can do nothing on its own power. There are many totalitarian ideas and ideologies that never move beyond just being ideas, remaining the obsession of a small group of adherents or the fixation of random professors and eccentrics. But some of these ideas do become entwined with organizations and movements, where groups of people work to bring these ideologies into practical reality. In the next chapter, it is to these movements that we turn our attention.

Summing Up

- A defining part of totalitarian ideology is its *totalism*, where the ideology (at least potentially) applies to all parts of human life, and perhaps even to the physical world.
- Most totalitarian ideologies think in terms of "History": that certain dynamics (economics, biology, or the like) drive human society toward a certain end state. "World-historic" populations are the "instruments" of these dynamics.
- In this worldview, the result of the dynamics of History is the creation of a fundamentally different – and better – "New Society," which will also create a "New Man": a new and advanced form of humanity.

Suggested Readings

There are various works that discuss totalitarian ideologies in general, and a substantial amount of literature focusing on specific types of totalitarian ideology. For the general types of discussion, useful works include Shorten (2012), Roberts (2006), and Ohana (2009). Turning to specific types of totalitarian ideologies, see Walicki (1995) and Kołakowski (2005), who provide nice overviews of Marxian-style ideology; Griffin (1991) and Gregor (2005) for more nationalistic forms of totalitarianism; and Weikart (2004) and Pichot (2009) for racialist ideologies. For a most interesting examination of Salafi-jihadism, see Maher (2016).

When studying these types of ideologies, it is also prudent to read the works of those who believe in them (although these texts are not always the most straightforward). For various types of Communism, useful texts would include Lenin (1987), Stalin (2002), and Mao (2007). For Fascism, one could read Mussolini (2006: 227–240), supplemented with Schnapp (2000), as well as Codreanu (2003). For Nazism, Hitler (1999[1927]) would be the primary text, which could be supplemented with Baynes (2006) and Stackelberg and Winkle (2002). For Islamism, useful texts would include Euben and Zaman (2009), as well as Kepel and Milelli (2008). Additional primary texts of possible use would include Gramsci (1971), Fanon (1963), Newton (1973), Pierce (2012), Symbionese Liberation Army 2019), and various the selections in Alexander and Pluchinsky (1992).

Notes

1. For those familiar with the Christian New Testament, this notion comes up in Matthew 24:36, "But about that day and hour no one knows, not even the angels in heaven, nor the Son, but the Father alone" (NASB).
2. Griffin (2007); Shorten (2012); Ben-Ghiat (2001); Halberstam (1999).
3. The term "millenarianism" originates within Christianity (referring to ideas/movements that believe the end of the world, and the final victory of God, is coming soon), but has also been used to describe other ideas/movements outside of Christianity. Norman Cohn identifies five overlapping traits in millenarianism, specifically that these movements "always picture salvation as (a) collective . . . (b) terrestrial . . . (c) imminent . . . (d) total . . . (e) miraculous" (Cohn 1970: 13).
4. See Cohn (1970).
5. See Voegelin (1997); Wiser (1980).
6. Piekalkiewicz and Penn (1995): 26–27.
7. See, among others, Ings (2016); Birstein (2001).
8. Mao (1972).
9. Hitler (1999[1927]).

10. Beyond *Mein Kampf*, some might point to Alfred Rosenberg's (2011[1937]) *Myth of the Twentieth Century* as a central text for Nazi ideology. While this book may be illuminating for some aspects of the Nazi worldview, various historians have noted that it appears most Nazis (much less the regular public) thought little of book itself, and its influence was minimal at best.

11. Kershaw (1999): 250.

12. By "reductive and truistic," I mean things that may indeed be true, but are also irrelevant. For instance, it would be true to say that your choice of a spouse is fundamentally caused by an extended conglomeration of chemical reactions within your body and in interaction with outside stimuli. But that statement tells us nothing regarding *who* and/or *why* you specifically chose that person, and even an outsider observer with access to all your internal chemical reactions would have no real clue about your choice based simply on chemistry.

13. Among others, see Jordan and Ip (2013).

14. Myers (2011).

15. For Hegel, what he thought drove History can be a matter of some scholarly debate, which we can leave to the side here. I am inclined to follow A. James Gregor's view that "Hegelianism is an all but impenetrable philosophical system, for which there is no single universally accepted interpretation, much less an acknowledged roster of all its real or fancied social or political implications" (Gregor 2012: 16).

16. See various of the chapters in Schnapp (2000).

17. See Gray (2020).

18. Engels (2008).

19. My thanks to Hassan Bashir for bringing the similarities between these two forms to my attention.

20. Within the scholarly (as well as popular) literature, multiple names are used to describe these types of ideologies and movements. Some have called them "jihadist" (Roy 2017; Khosrokhavar 2009), others "Islamo-fascist," and still others "salafi-jihadist" (Maher 2016), among the various names used. For simplicity's sake, we will follow Mozaffari's usage of "Islamism" (2017) for this book.

21. For an interesting discussion of Islamic political thought in its development, see Crone (2004).

22. Qutb (2002): 80.

23. A useful comparison would be with Marxian and social democratic thought in Europe in the late nineteenth and early twentieth centuries. It was not at all atypical that conversations – and even group-level cooperation – would exist between "revisionist" Marxists (more similar to contemporary social democrats), "mainstream" Marxists (like the German Social Democratic Party under Karl Kautsky), and extremists like Lenin and the Bolshevik party. It is possible that environmentalist ideology is in a similar position now.

24. For the ALF, see Animal Liberation Front (2011). For the ELF, see Pickering (2007). For EF!, see Davis (1991). For Kaczynski, see Kaczynski (2010). For a good general overview, see Liddick (2006).

25. Here, again, a religious comparison is apt. This change that is negative itself but also leads to a final positive is quite similar to some Christian notions of original sin: that the sin itself caused the "fall" of humanity away from paradise, but also served as a "*felix culpa*" (happy fault) leading to eternal salvation through the intervention of Christ. Although the categorization of totalitarianism as "political religion" is controversial and can have problems, the overlaps (borrowings?) of totalitarian thinking with religious thought are considerable.
26. Tackett (2015): 121.

Bibliography

Alexander, Yonah, and Dennis Pluchinsky (eds.). 1992. *Europe's Red Terrorists: The Fighting Communist Organizations*. New York: Frank Cass.

Animal Liberation Front. 2011. *Underground: The Animal Liberation Front in the 1990s*. No Location: Warcry Communications.

Baynes, Norman H. (ed.). 2006. *Speeches of Adolf Hitler: Early Speeches, 1922–1924, and Other Selections*. New York: Howard Fertig.

Ben-Ghiat, Ruth. 2001. *Fascist Modernities: Italy, 1922–1945*. Berkeley: University of California Press.

Birstein, Vadim J. 2001. *The Perversion of Knowledge: The True Story of Soviet Science*. Cambridge: Westview Press.

Codreanu, Corneliu Zelea. 2003. *For My Legionaries (The Iron Guard)*. Third Edition. York, SC: Liberty Bell Publications.

Cohn, Norman. 1970. *The Pursuit of the Millennium: Revolutionary Millenarians and Mystical Anarchists of the Middle Ages*. Revised and Expanded Edition. Oxford: Oxford University Press.

Crone, Patricia. 2004. *God's Rule, Government, and Islam: Six Centuries of Medieval Islamic Political Thought*. New York: Columbia University Press.

Davis, John (ed.). 1991. *The Earth First! Reader: Ten Years of Radical Environmentalism*. Salt Lake City: Peregrine Smith Book.

Engels, Friedrich. 2008. *Socialism: Utopian and Scientific*. Third Edition. Atlanta: Pathfinder Press.

Euben, Roxanne L., and Muhammad Qasim Zaman (eds.). 2009. *Princeton Readings in Islamist Thought: Texts and Contexts from al-Banna to Bin Laden*. Princeton: Princeton University Press.

Fanon, Frantz. 1963. *The Wretched of the Earth*. Constance Farrington, trans. New York: Grove Press.

Gramsci, Antonio. 1971. *Selections from the Prison Notebooks of Antonio Gramsci*. Quintin Hoare and Geoffrey Nowell Smith, eds., trans. New York: International Publishers.

Gray, Phillip W. 2020. *Vanguardism: Ideology and Organization in Totalitarian Politics*. New York: Routledge.

Gregor, A. James. 2005. *Mussolini's Intellectuals: Fascist Social and Political Thought*. Princeton: Princeton University Press.

Gregor, A. James. 2012. *Totalitarianism and Political Religion: An Intellectual History*. Stanford: Stanford University Press.

Griffin, Roger. 1991. *The Nature of Fascism*. London: Routledge.

Griffin, Roger. 2007. *Modernism and Fascism: The Sense of Beginning under Mussolini and Hitler*. New York: Palgrave Macmillan.

Halberstam, Michael. 1999. *Totalitarianism and the Modern Conception of Politics*. New Haven: Yale University Press.

Hitler, Adolf. 1999[1927]. *Mein Kampf*. Ralph Manheim, trans. Boston: Mariner Books.

Ings, Simon. 2016. *Stalin and the Scientists: A History of Triumph and Tragedy 1905–1953*. New York: Atlantic Monthly Press.

Jordan, Sara R., and Eric C. Y. Ip. 2013. "Demystifying the Hermit Kingdom: The Constitution and Public Administration in North Korea." *International Review of Administrative Sciences* 79(3): 544–562.

Kaczynski, Theodore J. 2010. *Technological Slavery: The Collected Writings of Theodore J. Kaczynski, a.k.a. "the Unabomber"*. Port Townsend: Feral House.

Kepel, Gilles, and Jean-Pierre Milelli (eds.). 2008. *Al Qaeda in Its Own Words*. Cambridge, MA: Belknap Press.

Kershaw, Ian. 1999. "'Working Towards the Führer': Reflections on the Nature of the Hitler Dictatorship." In Christian Leitz (ed.), *The Third Reich: The Essential Readings*. Malden, MA: Blackwell Publishing, pp. 233–252.

Khosrokhavar, Farhad. 2009. *Inside Jihadism: Understanding Jihadi Movements Worldwide*. London: Routledge.

Kołakowski, Leszek. 2005. *Main Currents of Marxism: The Founders, the Golden Age, the Breakdown*. P. S. Falla, trans. New York: W. W. Norton & Company.

Lenin, V. I. 1987. *Essential Works of Lenin: "What Is to Be Done?" and Other Writings*. H. M. Christman, ed. New York: Dover Publications.

Liddick, Donald R. 2006. *Eco-Terrorism: Radical Environmental and Animal Liberation Movements*. Westport: Praeger.

Maher, Shiraz. 2016. *Salafi-Jihadism: The History of an Idea*. Oxford: Oxford University Press.

Mao, Tse-Tung. 1972. *Quotations from Chairman Mao*. Peking: Foreign Language Press.

Mao, Tse-Tung. 2007. *On Practice and Contradiction*. London: Verso.

Mozaffari, Mehdi. 2017. *Islamism: A New Totalitarianism*. Boulder: Lynne Rienner Publishers.

Mussolini, Benito. 2006. *My Autobiography, with "the Political and Social Doctrine of Fascism"*. Richard Washburn Child and Jane Soamers, trans. Mineola: Dover Publications.

Myers, B. R. 2011. *The Cleanest Race: How North Koreans View Themselves: And Why It Matters*. Brooklyn: Melville House.

Newton, Huey P. 1973. *Revolutionary Suicide*. New York: Penguin Books.

Ohana, David. 2009. *The Dawn of Political Nihilism: Volume I of the Nihilist Order*. Brighton: Sussex Academic Press.

Pichot, André. 2009. *The Pure Society: From Darwin to Hitler*. David Fernbach, trans. London: Verso.

Pickering, Leslie James. 2007. *The Earth Liberation Front: 1997–2002*. Portland: Arissa Media Group.

Piekalkiewicz, Jaroslaw, and Alfred Wayne Penn. 1995. *Politics of Ideocracy*. Albany: State University of New York Press.

Pierce, William L. 2012. *Who We Are*. No Location: Revisionist Books.

Qutb, Sayyid. 2002. *Milestones*. New Delhi: Islamic Book Services (P) Ptd.

Roberts, David D. 2006. *The Totalitarian Experiment in Twentieth-Century Europe: Understanding the Poverty of Great Politics*. London: Routledge.

Rosenberg, Alfred. 2011[1937]. *The Myth of the Twentieth Century: An Evaluation of the Spiritual-Intellectual Confrontations of Our Age*. Wentzville, MO: Invictus Books.

Roy, Oliver, 2017. *Jihad and Death: The Global Appeal of Islamic State*. Cynthia Schoch, trans. Oxford: Oxford University Press.

Schnapp, Jeffrey T. (ed.). 2000. *Primer of Italian Fascism*. Lincoln, NE: University of Nebraska.

Shorten, Richard. 2012. *Modernism and Totalitarianism: Rethinking the Intellectual Sources of Nazism and Stalinism, 1945 to the Present*. London: Palgrave Macmillan.

Stackelberg, Roderick, and Sally A. Winkle (eds.). 2002. *The Nazi Germany Sourcebook: An Anthology of Texts*. London: Routledge.

Stalin, Joseph V. 2002. *Selected Works*. Honolulu: University Press of the Pacific.

Symbionese Liberation Army. 2019. *Death to the Fascist Insect*. John Brian King, ed. No Location: Spurl Editions.

Tackett, Timothy. 2015. *The Coming of the Terror in the French Revolution*. Cambridge: Belknap Press.

Voegelin, Eric. 1997. *Science, Politics and Gnosticism: Two Essays*. Washington, DC: Regnery Publishing, Inc.

Walicki, Andrzej. 1995. *Marxism and the Leapt to the Kingdom of Freedom: The Rise and Fall of the Communist Utopia*. Stanford: Stanford University Press.

Weikart, Richard. 2004. *From Darwin to Hitler: Evolutionary Ethics, Eugenics, and Racism in Germany*. New York: Palgrave Macmillan.

Wiser, James L. 1980. "From Cultural Analysis to Philosophical Anthropology: An Examination of Voegelin's Concept of Gnosticism." *Review of Politics* 42(1): 92–104.

MOVEMENT/PARTY
How Totalitarianism Organizes

An ideology may be totalitarian, but without a population sup-
porting it, the ideas remain politically irrelevant. When one looks
through history, there are quite a few ideologies that look pretty
totalitarian that don't end up going anywhere, with a few small bands
of adherents debating among themselves but not doing much else. If
you have attended some college campuses, you might have encoun-
tered this type of thing, with small groups focused on rather esoteric
and narrow views ("We are a collective of post-scarcity libertarian
communists," "I am a neo-reaction Evola-influenced minimarchist,"
or other such things). These types of fixations can be rather disconcerting, but generally have little broader impact, seeming more like
a trivial obsession similar to fantasy football or Marvel versus DC
comic-book debates, but just more jargon-filled. Ideas and ideologies
are important, but they are only one part of any ideational system.
This is especially true for totalitarianism. For totalitarian ideas to have
influence, they need a movement to go forward.

Historically, these movements are not purely spontaneous. In other
words, it is not as if a sizeable part of the population in Germany
woke up one morning in 1933, collectively thought "say, that small-
mustached guy seems like an up-and-up fellow," went out into the
street and demanded that the fellow, his ideology, and his party get
complete and total political power. Instead, these movements are
pushed, and sometimes explicitly headed, by a revolutionary party.
Spreading an ideology and gaining power cannot simply be a matter
of talking or writing. There is a need for organization and coordination, as even a large group of similarly minded people need some way
to ensure, for instance, that protests are held at the right time, that

DOI: 10.4324/9781003254232-3

information can spread to numerous places at once, and that potential candidates for leadership (political or otherwise) can be identified. This need for organization is true for any type of politics in the contemporary world, regardless of whether it is totalitarian, democratic, authoritarian, or something else. Is there, then, anything unique that distinguishes a totalitarian organization/movement from others, other than its ideology? Indeed, there are differences, which makes sense. It would be rather surprising if the shape of an organization was not influenced by the ideas one follows. But, additionally, as we will see, organizational structure can also shape parts of the ideology. Looking back to the examples of history, we do see a typical type of structure associated with totalitarian movements, which is based on the idea of the "world-historic" population (however defined) taking center stage, with its "advanced wing" taking the lead. V. I. Lenin – one of the most important figures of the twentieth century, founder of the Soviet Union, brilliant political thinker, highly dedicated, exceptionally intelligent, and very evil – referred to this group as the "*avant-garde*," more typically called the "vanguard party."[1] When considering how totalitarianism organizes itself, we need to keep the interactions between ideology, party, and movement in mind.

When looking at totalitarianism as a movement/organization, it is necessary to be somewhat cautious. The quantity of movements/organizations that could be considered totalitarian vastly outnumbers the number of totalitarian regimes that have existed. This can create a bit of a conceptualization issue. If a movement or organization never actually gains (much less maintains) political power, can one really be confident in calling that movement "totalitarian"? As noted in Chapter 1, totalitarianism is a term that can be thrown around rather loosely, especially against groups/movements one does not like. For our purposes, the examples in this chapter will primarily concentrate on two types of totalitarian movements/parties. First, many of the examples will focus upon movements/parties that would indeed gain power and create totalitarian regimes. The obvious benefit of these examples is that we have historical instances of what these movements did when in power. The second type of example will focus upon organizations/movements that show pretty consistent and clear totalitarian traits, leaning particularly heavily on these movements' ideologies, as well as their similarities to other movements that did indeed create totalitarian regimes. While perhaps not the most rigorous manner of addressing these concerns, it should be sufficient for our purposes in this text.

In this chapter, we will provide a general introduction to the manners in which totalitarianism organizes itself, except for its organization when it controls a government (that will be the subject of Chapter 4). Specifically, we will look at four elements of this topic. The first section will talk about the importance and role of mass politics (and mass society) in making totalitarian organization a possibility. Next, we will consider the role of the party. While almost every type of modern political system will have political parties of some type, totalitarian parties have shown a historical proclivity toward a specific, "vanguardist" form of political organization. Third, we will examine the role of movements more generally for totalitarianism. One of the disturbing things about totalitarianism is that it often aligns itself with other, less extreme political movements, and can eventually steer the movement in its own preferred direction. Finally, we will reflect upon the importance of crisis for totalitarianism to go from a movement seeking power to an organization with control over government. So, settle in. We have a great deal to cover in a short amount of space. First, we need to look at the type of society itself that is conducive to totalitarian movements: mass society.

Mass Politics

As noted in Chapter 1, totalitarianism is a pretty recent phenomenon. Many of the peculiarities of this type of politics depend upon certain social and material conditions that just did not exist in the period before about the eighteenth century or later. Among these conditions and factors, totalitarianism seems to require a type of "mass politics" as an environment in which to operate. By "mass politics," I mean a social structure in which large parts of the population are involved in political affairs, but are engaged in politics primarily as members of an identified social/political group rather than as individuals or simply citizens.[2] Let's break this definition down a bit. "Involved in public affairs" is pretty broad, and intentionally so. "Mass politics" does not mean that the average citizen acts as an official in the government or is directly voting on specific laws (as you might see in the ancient Greek city-state of Athens during its democratic period). Rather, "involved" means a feeling of engagement and concern about, interest in, and at least a potential sense of being able to influence political events.

It is the second half of this definition that is particularly important: "engaged in politics primarily as members of an identified social/political group." Unlike a small setting where one's engagement in political discussions is as an individual ("Theodore Rumpelstiltskin") or as representing a family ("the clan of Rumpelstiltskin") – for instance, in the "town halls" of northeastern North America in the eighteenth century[3] or the traditional *obshchina* of rural Russia[4] – in mass politics, individuals engage in politics as members/parts of large aggregate populations ("masses"). Moreover, it is in being a part of this "mass" that people can gain some sort of political voice, influence, and power. As a single person, Juan Garcia – a factory worker in occupation, Hispanic in ethnicity, Roman Catholic in religion – is merely one person in a political sea of 130 million people in his country. Without large wealth and connections, he lacks any real political voice or engagement. But Juan Garcia as one of 20 million Hispanics, 35 million Catholics, or 50 million factory workers has a *great* deal of influence due to these groups' collective engagement as aggregate populations. It is this fact – the amassing of political influence or power through the collective action of large subpopulations – that encapsulates the core of mass politics.

But we do need to narrow things down a little more, as we are specifically concerned with mass politics as an element of modern society. After all, there are multiple instances of large subpopulations influencing politics in earlier periods as well. Indeed, one of the reasons many ancient philosophers (such as Plato and Aristotle) had rather negative views about democracy arose from the detrimental influence of "mob rule" on laws and policies. In city-states, especially in republican Rome, masses of the population could radically shift the balance of power in a government, especially during periods of crisis.[5] Were these cases of "mass politics" in the pre-modern period? While these types of "mob politics" share notable similarities to "mass politics," there are three differences that are particularly relevant for our discussion. First, mass politics involves a scale of population and engagement that was simply not possible in earlier periods. If estimates just after the rise of Augustus Caesar are correct, Rome had a population of about 4 million people in 28 BC/BCE. Let's compare that with the population of Italy in 1922 (the year of the

Fascists' "March on Rome"), which was estimated to be 38 million people. The sheer size of population has changed markedly between the modern period and earlier eras, and we can safely hypothesize that a larger percentage of Italy's 1922 population was engaged in politics in comparison to Rome's population under Augustus.

This greater level of engagement brings us to the second, and more relevant, difference: the spread of information and communication. Even in the most advanced of ancient cities the literate usually made up a small fraction of the population, and information spread very slowly. Even along road-connected, land-based areas, getting news from a town 100 miles away would take a significant amount of time, and this lag increased substantially if one had to cross wilderness, seas, or other obstacles. Within the modern period, on the other hand, literacy rates increased greatly, and the speed of information grew exponentially. Rather than taking weeks or months to find out information from the other side of the continent or around the world, advancements in communication (including the telegraph, radio, television/film, and the rapidity of delivery via railroads, cars, advanced ships at sea, and airplanes) meant news could spread – and have an effect – within days or even minutes. So, going back to the example of Italy, it would have taken a great deal of time for people in various parts of Roman territory to learn of Augustus Caesar's rule, in contrast to people across Italy (and indeed, around the world) hearing about the March on Rome within hours at the most.

Third, and finally, the decay of earlier forms of identification allowed the aggregate populations in modernity to form into mass politics as we know it. Related to smaller populations and less developed forms of communication and travel, the forms of identity and connections in earlier periods tended to be local: traditional connections to home and extended family, to local customs and laws, and indeed to local forms of leadership and ruling authority. Even those forms of identity that extended beyond one's local area typically had significant elements of "local flavor" that would distinguish them. A good example from medieval Europe would be the importance, and variety, of local saints among Catholic populations. While identifying with a universalist religion, people would also feel a connection with local variations as identified by specific saints (such as St. Thomas Beckett in England, or Saint Armel in Ploërmel, France). Technological development, especially during the Industrial Revolution, weakened these types of identity in major ways. With changes in productive technology (such as with textiles, among many others) as well as in the increased centralization by states,[6] large segments of the rural and subsistence farmer populations moved into the cities for a more regular income, among other things. Homes where families had lived for generations now emptied; connections and norms between families formed over hundreds of years dissolved into the mass of strangers colliding into each other within larger cities and a sense of lived connection to the past (through the land one worked) gave way to the *anomie* of the anonymous, often dirty and dangerous, city streets. As humans are rather social creatures, new forms of identity would almost be formed by necessity. Within the new cities, sometimes this arose as a matter of affiliating with one's neighborhood, but, in practice, other types of identity would prevail: identities based upon economic class, based upon ethnic identity, based upon national origin, and (especially when looking to the developing world and the Middle East) based upon religion. As local/particular types of identity retreat into the horizon, more extended and universal forms of mass identity take their place.

That the "masses" of society are involved in politics, however, is only part of the equation. Of central importance, in mass politics generally and for totalitarianism specifically, is the role of *organization*. Outside of some very limited circumstances, a large group of people cannot coordinate its activities on its own and spontaneously. Think of your own experiences of being with a group. It is not atypical for an assemblage of, say, 11 friends to decide they want to "do something," but they will often stand around and asking each other "what do you want to do?" until one or two friends take the lead to say "we're heading to movies" or what have you. If this problem exists among 11 people, it becomes rather more daunting with 1,100 people or 11,000 people, and even more so with 11 million people. Mass politics is not merely the engagement of a larger part of society, but also effective the direction, control, and coordination of these populations. Organization involves setting up lines of communication and creating certain standard operating procedures (SOPs) – be they formal or informal – that offer predictability in actions, clarifying who should be doing what, but especially providing leadership. For organizations in mass politics, leadership takes on many forms and arises at various levels. While much more rigorous than most mass political organizations, we can give the military as an example. If we think of a military leader, perhaps General George S. Patton (1885–1945) of the United States comes to mind, or at least the character of Patton as performed by George C. Scott in 1970. Yes, it is Gen. Patton who is giving overall directions, providing inspiration for the troops, and arranging that necessary equipment (bullets, tanks, food, and the like) are available for his men. But there are other types of leaders needed in order for Gen. Patton's army to succeed. His advisors and staff handle the administrative details to get his plans in place, quartermasters arrange the specifics of getting materials to troops, lower-level officers (lieutenants and captains) direct the troops on the battlefield, non-commissioned officers (sergeants) direct the infantry and front-line soldiers in their specific missions. For Gen. Patton to succeed, he needs to be a good leader, but he also needs an organizational structure and a slew of additional, lower-level leaders in order to see his plans put in place. So too with an organization in mass politics. These groups will have main leaders that the general public (or at least the run-of-the-mill organization members) will know, but these leaders need an organizational infrastructure to make any progress – administrators who ensure that funds are going to the right parts of the organization at the right time, fundraisers collecting funds by one means or another, writers/popularizers using various media (print, radio, TV, or now the internet) to spread the organization's ideas, editorial leaders who ensure that the writers/popularizers are on "the same page" in providing messages consistent with the organization's ideas and aims, and organizers at the local level who mobilize parts of the aggregate population to join the group and/ or participate in marches/protests to operate successfully. Even if the movement bases itself upon the notions of full equality or the like, its organization (to be successful) will by necessity require some levels of hierarchy and leadership.[7]

Whether one is dealing with democratic, authoritarian, or totalitarian forms of political engagement, these organizations pay particular attention on how best to structure themselves for political victory. Among the types of organizations formed, many of these movements (regardless of regime type or motivation) often aim to make a political party. Totalitarian movements often (historically) gravitate toward a specific type of party, which can be broadly described as the "vanguard party." It is to this system we now turn.

The Party

One of the central organizational elements for totalitarianism, at least historically, has been the creation and expansion of a party dedicated to creating a new system. While trying to mobilize an aggregate/mass population, the "core" of totalitarians maintains an unrelenting focus on the final aim of social revolution and the radical change of society. To make this change requires organization from a dedicated group of revolutionaries. In the words of Abdallah Azzam, one of the founders of Al-Qaeda, "Every dogma, even if it comes from the Lord of the worlds, will be stillborn if it does not find a vanguard that sacrifices itself and expends every effort in order to defend it."[8] This dedicated group becomes the center of the totalitarian political party. Political parties obviously make up a significant part of politics in liberal democracies, whether it is the Republicans and Democrats in the United States, the Conservatives and Labour in the United Kingdom, or Liberal Democratic Party and the Constitutional Democratic Party in Japan. In our age of mass politics, these parties arrange themselves as discussed in the previous section, and primarily aim to win public office through elections. These parties may seek other types of influence – for instance, encouraging certain industries or other parts of society to act on their own to further the party's aims – but electoral victory usually is the highest end. The totalitarian party is something significantly different from these other parties in three ways.

First, the totalitarian party generally denies (even if *sotto voce*) the legitimacy of the political system in which it operates, seeking to gain power to eradicate the current system and replace it with their own. Whether by insurrection, civil war, or through the "strategic" use of elections (called the "path of legality" in Nazi circles, as mentioned in Chapter 2), the totalitarian party seeks complete control to create absolute and total change. This is in strong contrast to typical political parties in liberal democracies, where the parties recognize and affirm the inherent legitimacy of their constitutional systems, even if a party may want to make substantial changes. If one wants to use somewhat fancier language, one could say that typical political parties accept the current system normatively (in other words, that as a matter of values and principles, they believe the governing system to be legitimate), while totalitarian parties engage in the current system "strategically" (in other words, they work within the current political system by necessity, but will jettison that system as soon as the party can eliminate it). Once a totalitarian political party attains enough power (through one means or another) to direct the government, it stops pretending to give the previous system any legitimacy and will instead actively (and loudly) denounce it and attempt to completely destroy it.

Second, most totalitarian parties will often take the shape of a "vanguard" party.[9] The "vanguard party" is usually associated with Lenin, as he was its major theoretician as well as the leader of the first vanguard party to actually succeed in taking over a political system (the Bolshevik party, later Communist Party). However, the vanguard party structure has been used by various types of totalitarians and is not limited to Communists or Marxist-Leninists. While there are various elements to a vanguard party, we will discuss some of the most important ones here. As its name implies, the party is made of the *avant-garde* of the "world-historic" population. The party is supposed to be the "tip of the spear" and the "most advanced" part of this population, guiding it toward its Historical destiny of radically changing society. Think back to the discussion in Chapter 2 about "world-historic" populations. The vanguard party views itself as the part of this population that helps direct it along its way. The vanguard party usually also creates and/or harbors "professional revolutionaries," whose sole job and focus is on advancing the totalitarian party to victory. Unlike the rest of the "world-historic" population – people who have jobs, families, and/or suffer under "false consciousness" – the "professional revolutionaries" know the "science" of History and have dedicated their full time and energy to the social revolution. For totalitarians, professional revolutionaries can act in ways that the aggregate population – the mass, the "world-historic" population, and the like – simply lacks the capacity to do. Lenin provides a good summation of this view (even if it is a bit of a longer quote):

Such workers, average people of the masses, are capable of displaying enormous energy and self-sacrifice in strikes and in street battles with the police and the troops, and are capable (in fact, are alone capable) of *determining* the outcome of our entire movement – but the struggle against the political police requires special qualities; it requires *professional* revolutionaries. And we must see to it, not only that the masses 'advance' concrete demands, but that the masses of workers 'advance' an increasing number of professional revolutionaries.[10]

As Lenin notes, one of the aims of the vanguard's "professional revolutionaries" is to spawn more of themselves. In a sense, a "critical mass" of these professional revolutionaries could make the difference between an opportunity for revolution being successful or instead "fizzling out" (because of lack of direction, lack of support, or the like). This vanguard party may sound rather elitist, and indeed it is, to a certain extent. But a core trait of vanguard parties is their self-perceived relation to the "world-historic" population. This vanguard sincerely believes it is just the advanced tip of the full population, and the party's legitimacy, energy, and authority come from the "world-historic" population. Without this connection to the population (at least in their own minds), the vanguard party would not be a "vanguard" at all, but instead a group of adventurers with delusions of grandeur, acting more like "utopians" who think they can change the world by force of will/morals rather than by following the dynamics of History. It is this connection to the "mass" that distinguishes a vanguard party from a completely elitist form of organization. For something like an aristocracy (rule by "the best," but in practice a type of hereditary leadership) or a technocracy (rule by "science" or "experts," but in practice a type of leadership by those with the "correct" credentials), there is a sense of noblesse oblige (the notion that those of a higher station have a responsibility for the wellbeing of the lower orders), with the idea being that the "better" people have an obligation to assist the "peasants" or the "stupid" (depending in the type). This notion does not really exist within the movement stages of a vanguard party, as the vanguard views itself as totally dependent upon the mass of the world-historic population for its very existence.

A third major difference between totalitarian party organization and most regular political parties deals with political violence. Can violence be used to bring about political/social changes? Obviously, this is a rather touchy subject on many levels. Most people would denounce violence as a form of political activity unless it is something really, *really* important to those people, in which case violence might be acceptable. Naturally, it is typical for people to denounce violence committed by those viewed as political opponents or enemies (seeing these acts as completely and totally unjustified) while violence committed by political allies or "fellow travelers" will often be excused (it was an "excess" caused by righteous indignation) or even supported. In more stable political systems, political parties usually make it a point to explicitly reject violence as a means to gain political power (even if they may "wink at" some of it). Totalitarian parties, on the other hand, do not reject political violence. As many of their ideologies focus rather strongly on the idea that violent overthrow of the governing system is a key part of the social revolution (it is a rare thing for a revolution *not* to involve bloodshed), the importance of violence is "baked in," as it were, to their view of reality. In practice, these totalitarian parties often will form their own "paramilitary" units: armed, organized cadres used for "extralegal" activities that can run the gamut from acting as security for party events to roughing up people on the streets (such as members of the "Enemy" population, as well as other paramilitary units from other extremist groups) to murder. These parties will often claim these paramilitary units are for strictly "defensive" purposes. In Weimar Germany, the original "purpose" of the Nazi Party's *Sturmabteilung* (SA, usually translated as "Stormtroopers") was to act as security against Communist extremists who would interrupt party events and beat up attendees, and the German Communist Party's (KPD) paramilitary *Antifaschistische Aktion* (usually translated simply as "Antifa") as a "defense" against Fascist and Nazi extremists.[11] As totalitarian parties view themselves in a totalistic war against the current form of society, they are comfortable with the use of violence for political ends. For them, violence becomes an issue if it is used poorly rather than if it is used at all. Violence should not lead to the party being hurt (for instance, if the party is made illegal after a member murders an opposing political party's leader), but instead should advance the party (say, by "encouraging" people in a specific neighborhood to vote the "correct" way to avoid getting beaten up in the streets). Totalitarian parties often have a rather instrumentalist view of violence, as there is no moral "content" to violence outside of the broader aims of social revolution. If shooting children in front of their mothers slows down the advance of the social revolution, it is wrong; but if shooting children in front of their mothers would bring about the victorious social revolution more quickly, it is *good and praiseworthy* for the totalitarian party to shoot them.

Viewed from the outside, the totalitarian party does not sound like a group most people would want as an associate or ally. If they remained simply on their own, most totalitarian parties would likely get few adherents. However, as part of a broader movement, totalitarians have greater opportunities for influence, new members, and power.

Movements and Totalitarian Parties

Historically, the vanguard party has been an essential part of totalitarianism's success. But we have also historically seen that even well-organized and well-funded vanguards cannot get anywhere near success without a movement. "Movement" is yet another word that can have multiple meanings – ah, the joys of political analysis. For our purposes, we will define social movements as a "distinct social process, consisting of the mechanisms through which actors engage[] in collective action: are involved in conflictual relations with clearly defined opponents[;] are linked by dense informal networks[;] share a distinct collective identity."[12] Great. So what does that all mean? One thing to note immediately is that "movement" covers a much broader area than an organization or a party. When people use the term "Civil Rights Movement" in the United States or "Solidarity Movement" in Poland, they are not simply using a short-hand phrase for the NAACP (in the USA) or the Independent Self-Governing Trade Union (in Poland). Usually, there is a significantly larger number of people who are willing to "side" with a movement than the people who identify themselves with a specific organization (much less are members of it).[13] As the definition notes, the central part of a movement is how it allows people to engage in collective actions and activities, usually to support (or prevent) some type of political, social, or similar change. For such collective activity to exist, there needs to be a "distinct collective identity." In other words, something that brings people to believe they are "unified" in something. It could be based on similarity in race, ethnicity, class, religion, regional or national identity, language, a shared ideology, or various other things, but it needs to be *something*. While organizations play an important (indeed, vital) role for movements to work, movements also need "dense informal networks" – the types of connections between people that do not depend on formal rules or administration. This would include informal interactions between different types of organizations (for instance, an explicitly political organization doing "under the table" coordinating of protests with a trade union), though more typically the forms of communication and connections that arise between people working in similar areas or on overlapping topics. Finally, movements almost always have a conflictual element to them, and in some cases the "collective identity" of the movement is shaped more by a shared notion of an opponent or enemy than by a unifying trait (something that will come up again when talking about totalitarianism in movements). A movement will always be *against* something, which may be rather abstract ("capitalism," "the State," "the foreign"), but will often focus on concrete targets as well (fixating on perhaps Andrew Carnegie, the Internal Revenue Service, or the Russians). People can often feel motivated when fighting against some force or entity, but, moreover, enemies bring unity. Groups that have very different ideas of what policies are preferrable may align with each other against another foe. If we look at American politics, much of the coalition in the Republican Party during the Cold War aligned on a shared focused of anti-communism, as this coalition included significant factions within it (social conservatives, libertarians, bigger businesses, and others) that disagreed significantly on what "should be" rather than what "should be fought."

An ongoing danger for nearly any political movement is the possibility of being overtaken by totalitarian-minded "professional revolutionaries" and their fellow travelers, as briefly noted at the end of Chapter 2. Looking historically, most of the vanguard parties that would end up taking control of a country did not, in themselves, start the mass political movements that brought them into power. Indeed, most of the people involved in these movements (especially those who were most actively engaged with it) early on would have laughed at the possibility. To them, the notion that the constantly infighting Bolsheviks or the comparatively low-member Nazis could take the reins of the movement would sound about as nonsensical as the idea of the homeless schizophrenic man in your town (who spends most of his time conversing with parking meters) soon becoming mayor. But over time, in these cases, the possibility of a totalitarian takeover of the movement no longer seemed funny, and was a realistic prospect. Various individuals or groups within these and other movements may try (but fail) to prevent the totalitarians from getting more influence. So, we need to ask why and how: *why* did some movements fall under the sway of totalitarian ideologies and parties? *How* did these ideologies and parties gain prominence?

In any mass movement, there will be a plethora of different groups, interests, and ideologies, which often range from the most moderate/ status quo-oriented to the most extreme/radical, with others filling in the area in-between. Which groups/interests/ideologies dominate at any given time reflects numerous factors. Some factors are organizational: groups with better funding, groups with more active members, and groups that are better at sloganeering/making memorable phrases/arguments will likely have more influence. Other factors are external. In generally stable societies with a high level of social trust/ peace, the more moderate/status-quo oriented groups will tend to dominate. In times of high instability and/or low social trust, on the other hand, circumstances will give the more extreme groups more influence. Finally, there are some factors that could be called individual or personal (or perhaps "personnel" might be more accurate): groups with highly dedicated members (even if small in number) or groups that have particularly notable or highly charismatic members/ leaders can have an outsized influence on which groups dominate in a movement. This last point is harder to pin down, as "charisma" is notoriously difficult to define and even harder to measure.[14] But this one is also rather intuitively obvious, as we usually associate a person with a movement: Martin Luther King Jr. in the Civil Rights Movement of the United States, Nelson Mandela in the anti-apartheid movement in South Africa, and Vaclav Havel with the Velvet Revolution movement in Czechoslovakia are just a few examples of this tendency.

The Bolshevik party in Tsarist Russia provides an excellent example of a group that had many of these factors, leading it to be far more influential than its raw numbers would indicate. In the Russian democratic and socialist movements, the Bolsheviks were a pretty small group, with a larger number of them living in other countries (to avoid the Okhrana, the Tsarist Russian secret police). However, they could rely on some helpful levels of funding – be it from membership fees, rich donors, or "expropriations" (a euphemism for armed robberies) – and its members tended to be highly dedicated. The influence of the Bolsheviks, in contrast to the Mensheviks and other parties, fluctuated with the status of Russian society itself. Bolsheviks were much more popular as domestic affairs degraded during the First World War, but tended to be just a fringe (varying between being despised and being ignored) in more peaceful and stable periods, such as during Russia's brief phase of constitutional monarchy from about 1905 until the war. These factors alone would make the Bolsheviks players of variable importance in the social movements of Russia, but the decisive factor would have to be personnel. It is hard to overstate the organizational, rhetorical, and energetic activity of members such as Lev Trotsky, Joseph Stalin, Nikolai Bukharin, and most especially Lenin. By being constantly active in pushing the party forward while also showing a shrewd understanding of using opportunities as they arose, the Bolshevik party's leadership was able to use the circumstances in late 1917 to take power for themselves. We can also see this in Germany, where the Nazi party went from an almost comical group of rabble-rousers in 1923 to the dominant force in German politics by 1933. Let's focus on one particular element of Nazi rhetoric that helped give them an edge against other groups in the German nationalist movement, specifically the use of an important yet ambiguous word. Unlike many of the other groups in the nationalist movement – which included restorationist conservatives (who wanted to bring back the rule of the Kaiser), Fascist-oriented groups (focused on cultural nationalism), and some *Völkisch* groups (with a "thicker" notion of nationalism) – the Nazi ideology was racialist in nature. A word, however, helped the Nazis solidify their position with many groups, including those that were not primarily racialist (or indeed, who did not focus on race much at all): *Volk*. In German, *Volk* is one of those words that is both straightforward but also rather equivocal. In English, it's usually translated as "folk," which is also a rather equivocal word, so obviously this does not clear things up terribly well. Depending on context or intention, *Volk* can mean many things. It can also be translated as "people" (as in *a* people – a specific population), "nation" (be it talking about a national culture or a "thicker" nationalism that includes culture, norms, language, and perhaps ancestry), and "race." Hegel used the word when talking about mass (usually national) populations as well as the "world-historic" population. *Volk* is a word that is important and yet is also rather slippery in its meaning. One of the great skills of Hitler and the Nazi party was their ability to play off this equivocality. When giving a speech to a broader audience, Hitler could discuss *Volk* in such a way that the audience would interpret it to "fit" with their own views. To some of the conservatives (many of them found Hitler too radical and low-class), *Volk* meant a return to the old system. For nationalists of various stripes, *Volk* meant the historical German nation. For racialists, *Volk* meant race. As each of these groups had numerous disputes between themselves, the Nazis could present themselves as speaking for the entire movement. And, in unstable circumstances, it could (and did) work. This does not mean that it was all just rhetoric with no substance. There was a quite developed racialist ideology in his Nazi ideas and speeches, but the Nazis excelled at publishing slogans and propaganda that could *sound* like it meant something less divisive until they gained power. When they were controlling the government, there was less of a need for such slippery use of language.

One other way this overtaking occurs is typically called "entryism." "Entryism" refers to when a group (it need not be totalitarian, but often is) seeks to put its members into an organization with broader (and usually less extreme) aims in order to place that organization under the group's control. A silly example might help. Imagine a city with a group of radical left-hand supremacists (let's call them the "Lefthanded Liberation Front," or "LLF") who believe that left-handed people are humanity's superiors and should rule society. Being a rather niche group, it has difficulty getting support and membership. One of the most popular and well-regarded organizations in the city is "Metro Knitting Association" (MKA), a knitting club that has numerous members from many backgrounds and tends to have a very favorable reputation among most people. The LLF decides it will try entryism. Some of its members join the MKA, being sure to hide their connections to the LLF and avoid "preaching" at the people in the knitting group. The LLF entryists act as dedicated members of the MKA, popularizing its activities, volunteering for various functions, and working their way into the organization and leadership. As they gain more organizational power, the entryists ensure more LLF members join the MKA. Subtly and over time, the entryist members start shifting the knitting club, perhaps arranging special days for left-handed knitters, dedicating resources to "celebrating left-handed knitters in history," and the like. They will also try to purge out elements from the association that go against their ideology. If the MKA's logo is two right hands shaking, the entryists in leadership will push to remove this "righthand-centric" and "big-oted" depiction. If successful, the entryists will completely change the nature of the organization. The broadly appealing knitting club has now become a subordinate affiliate of the LLF. For entryism to be truly successful, however, the MKA must still appear to be a completely unassociated group. Beyond being able to spread its ideology and policies through a "nonpartisan" association, the LLF can point to the MKA's actions as showing how "even these non-political groups" are onboard with the LLF's aims.

The typical historical example of "entryism" would be Communist (be it Marxist-Leninist, Trotskyist, or some other form) infiltration of certain unions or other groups. The Communist vanguard party – often viewed as on "the fringe" of the movement – decides that a few dedicated Communist Party members should join a trade union and conceal their membership with the Communists. Indeed, these members initially disavow any connection with the Communist Party and perhaps even make some criticisms of it. These "entryist" members are tasked with being good union members, with the aim of getting into positions of authority within the union. During this process, the "entryist" members may will attempt to "shift" the union more in the direction of the Communist Party, pushing more for radical structural changes rather than more narrow aims of increased pay and focusing more on showing "solidarity" with (Communist) revolutions in other countries and the like. If successful, the Communist Party will effectively control the union while simultaneously being able to claim that an "independent and respected" organization also happens to advocate for the same things as the Communists.[15] While the Communist example is the most straightforward, one can find instances where Fascists or racialists overtake patriotic nationalist associations and veterans' groups, among others.

So far, we have focused upon how totalitarian organizations try to subvert movements. But that also makes things a little too easy and simple. Again, life would be much simpler if totalitarians gained power simply because some evil men, twisting their handlebar moustaches and cackling at the sky like movie villains, were so overwhelming powerful, intelligent, or charismatic as to drag everyone along. That's a nice story we can tell ourselves – who could stand against SPECTRE or Hydra? – but it is a fiction. One major difficulty that movements can face is that various movement members can be too accommodating to the totalitarian extremists. For some, the totalitarians appear idealistic, or perhaps appear to be "pure" members of the movement, insofar as the totalitarians are less inclined toward compromising on their principles and demands. It is an unfortunate, but also highly typical, tendency for people to equate "more extreme" with "more authentic," and this occurs frequently within the history of totalitarianism's expansion within movements. Many within the movement will look at the totalitarian parts as having "good intentions" and that "their hearts are in the right place," but are viewed as too unrealistic in their aims. The mentality is often that "yes, the final end these people want – the classless society, the pure society, or whatever else – are commendable, and *of course* we want the same, in broad strokes. But this talk of social revolution or total control of society is just too impractical. We need to work on realistic goals, like changing labor laws or winning elections." This propensity for less-radical movement members to dismiss the totalitarian elements as a threat has an unfortunately long pedigree. We can see this tendency even as early as the French Revolution:

> If they rapidly grew impatient and intolerant with the opposition, their intolerance came from their fervent belief that the values in question were necessary for the new society they had come to envision and that patriots must be prepared to do whatever necessary to save the Revolution and preserve those gains.[16]

It is far from atypical to see this mentality form within a movement, especially if it seems to be succeeding.

One can see this tendency in some historic leftwing movements, where the implicit motto was "no enemies to the Left." In other words, movement members would tend to excuse or ignore actions (even violence) by the extremists within their ranks, as they believe all attention should be focused on the "true" enemies from the political Right. At most, other movement members might note disappointment in the "excesses" of the totalitarians, "contextualizing" violence as an understandable response to "aggressions" (always intentional and never a mere "excess") from the political system or their political opponents. It seems that some movement leaders believe this type of "winking at" the totalitarian elements can be useful, insofar as the leaders can portray themselves as the "reasonable" activists with whom others can work. In practice, however, the totalitarian elements can grow in influence as the most "authentic" part of the movement and the part that "gets things done." This problem exists even when the totalitarian elements come to power and form their own regimes, with many individuals and groups from other societies evincing a shocking level of (at best) willful blindness.[17]

Do all these factors together result in a totalitarian organization gaining control of a county? It has an ideology, it has its own (often vanguardist) organization, and it can tap into the collective strength of a broader movement. Is this enough? We could say that these factors are necessary but not sufficient for totalitarianism to obtain power. There is one other element that is almost always needed for victory, to which we now turn.

Crisis and Victory

Even with an ideology, a party, and a movement, there is still one other thing that appears necessary for totalitarianism to take control of a society: crisis.[18] I am hard-pressed to think of any instance of totalitarianism taking hold outside of a crisis situation. The necessity of crisis makes sense, intuitively. When things are generally going well, and day-to-day life is pleasant (or at least tolerable), most people have little inclination for radical, far-reaching changes. But if there are major economic downturns or social upheavals, or even major natural disasters, then more members of a society would be inclined to at least hear radical solutions.

As with so many of the terms used in this book, "crisis" is a term that is both broad and open to multiple interpretations. It is certainly a word in common usage to describe constitutional conflicts, wars, financial downturns, lack of parking when trying to get to a doctor's appointment or test, and the unexpected lack of coffee in one's pantry, among other things. The notion of "crisis" itself derives in many ways from ideas within medical thought in ancient Greece, where "crisis" was a central point in the progression of certain illnesses. When a "crisis" arises (say, when a patient has a high fever), the illness will "break" and the patient will start improving, or the illness will take a deep hold on the patient (likely resulting in death).[19] This old notion can help us in understanding crisis as it relates to totalitarianism. For a totalitarian party and movement to succeed in gaining power, the current political (and often social) system must be in a situation where its foundational legitimacy is in question, and where there is little time for the system to regain its authority. Crisis, in this sense, is a mixture of severity and a short timeframe.

In ordinary times, there will complaints about how the system operates – that it benefits some people over others, that it's inefficient, that it has corruption problems, or the like – but it can still operate. The broader part of the public sees these problems as "a few bad apples" in an otherwise good system (for instance), where some type of reforms are needed, but the system fundamentally is sound. In a crisis situation, on the other hand, larger parts of the public, and indeed even significant portions of the ruling groups themselves, start to believe the system is fundamentally corrupt, unjust, or unworkable. Crisis involves this deep distrust in the legitimacy of the existing system, but such a system can continue to exist for some time in such conditions. For instance, although the Roman Empire started suffering significant economic issues in the third century from which it never truly recovered, and its political leadership was in ongoing flux as various dictators fought it out, the Empire managed to still limp on for another two hundred years. The other important part of crisis for our purposes is a short timeframe. Not only is there a deep ambivalence (at best) toward the current system, but there is also a rather small amount of time for the system to seek ways to stabilize itself. So, going again to the Roman Empire example, while the legitimacy issues remained and the economy struggled along, it was generally gradual enough (and the political system spread out enough) to permit the Empire to continue existing for some time. For our sense of crisis, things are not gradual. Events that would shorten the timeframe would often include what one could call "existential" issues: issues that involve one's continued ability to live. Using the economy as an example, a gradual downturn – even if it is a long and unpleasant one – will generally not bring about a crisis, as residents in a system have time to find ways to adjust to the new realities. A catastrophic economic downturn, however, where large numbers of workers cannot find employment, many people lose their homes, and perhaps people even face issues of famine, can bring about a crisis in our sense. If people have to "tighten their belts" to adjust and buy less things, a system can survive such issues with some degree of success. If, on the other hand, people have to eat grass and tree bark just to live another day (so the public's timeframe isn't years or even months, but now a week or even a day), the system can only survive these problems through a quick solution or a major use of coercion. Other types of "existential" issues can include warfare (particularly for those individuals and families who have to fight the war), regional instability and separatism within a country, and many others.

But a shortened timeframe can also include actions that are psychologically or symbolically devastating. Using our earlier example, while the Roman Empire continued on through political instability and economic problems, it was sacking of Rome by the Visigoths in 410 AD/CE that truly brought about the final crisis of the Roman system, as the overtaking of the capital city was a major psychological blow to the Roman belief in their own invincibility. One could also look at the symbolic element of the 11 September 2001 attacks on the United States in a similar manner. The attacks themselves caused a great deal of death and destruction, but even more jarring for the public was what it symbolized. It had been decades – almost outside of living memory – since the United States had been attacked on its own territory in such a shattering fashion. For the Romans, the overtaking of Rome would lead to the Western Empire's demise in a few decades, as the Empire's legitimacy was already in question. For the Americans, the system could continue after the 9/11 attacks because the United States' fundamental authority was still recognized by most of the public. Each factor – loss of fundamental legitimacy or a major issue in a narrow timeframe – will bring problems, but it generally needs to be both together to create a crisis by which totalitarian movements can gain victory.

While we will note their historical importance in Chapter 5, there are two examples of such crises that would be useful to discuss here: the aftermath of the First World War and the results of the Iraq War in the early twenty-first century. It is important to note at the start that when considering these crises, it is not a matter of whether a particular war was just or unjust, wise or imprudent. It would be nice if crises only arose from bad actions from states, or as the "just desserts" for fighting some types of wars. Unfortunately, life is not a morality play where the good guys always win, the bad guys always lose, and the just always go on to live happily ever after. Countries can fight totally unjust wars without crises arising, and others can fight justified wars with the end result being the destruction of themselves. Our concern is to note some cases where wars brought about crisis situations that opened the door for totalitarian organizations to gain power. Let's look at each of these in turn.

The ideas, and indeed some of the organizations, that would be pivotal for later totalitarian regimes had formed, usually in embryonic form, before First World War (1914–1918). A wide variety of Marxian groups already existed by this point, and sundry types of anarchist, ultra-nationalist, racialist, and other ideas and groups were beginning to arise. How these various ideas and movements would have played out in the absence of the war is impossible to say, but one can state with great certainty that the crises caused by the war (directly or indirectly) created the circumstances for totalitarianism to take hold of numerous countries in the following 30 years. Most European countries faced crushing conditions during the First World War, with horrific levels of carnage among soldiers, massive levels of destruction in numerous parts of the continent, and substantial deprivation for noncombatants at home. These ongoing issues, as well as the often stalemate-like nature of trench warfare during the conflict, created crisis situations in numerous European countries. Moreover, the conflict was the first major instance of "total warfare," where entire societies are mobilized toward victory. Organizationally, total warfare lends itself to rigorous centralization with planning run by government agencies, an increase in administrative and executive branch decision-making (with a marked decrease in representative/democratic decision-making), strict implementation of policies and sanctions internally in the country, and a nearly fanatical fixation on a specific notion of efficiency (efficiency in winning the war) at the expense of other things. These changes focused on the "rational" planning of government activities, which also played a role in various ideologies at the time. Many of the existing regimes (be they representative democracies, monarchies of one form of another, or empires) were not well-equipped to handle these types of changes.

The most immediate and notable result of the First World War was the victory of Lenin's Bolsheviks (they called themselves the Communist Party in 1918, after their victory) during the "October Revolution" in 1917. For the first time in history, a totalitarian organization and movement managed to achieve full control over a country. The success of the Bolsheviks served as an inspiration to many other radicals in the aftermath of the war, which included various individuals and groups involved in the Bavarian Soviet Republic (1918–1919), the Hungarian Soviet Republic (1919), and others. But the war also strengthened other totalitarian tendencies in other areas. Societal and political chaos continued in Italy (for reasons discussed in Chapter 5), where Mussolini's Fascist party would portray itself as a "trenchocracy" (rule by the veterans of the war, who sacrificed for the nation) that could lead Italy out of crisis. In Germany, defeat in the war, the shaky legitimacy of the new Weimar Republic, and continued tensions with other nations (among other things) provided ample ground for various totalitarian parties and movements to gain traction, with the Nazi party finally gaining victory in 1933. It is rather unlikely that any of these totalitarian groups would have gained political power – or indeed, would have made much of an impression on history at all – had the war never occurred.

The Iraq War (2003–2011) provides another crisis example. In a region already known for tendency toward political instability, the balance of the Middle East was thrown into disarray with the war. While the dictator of Iraq – Saddam Hussein – had few people internally or externally who liked his regime, the removal of the government brought about numerous other problems. The ideology of Hussein's ruling party (the Arab Socialist Ba'ath Party) overlapped in many ways with both other national liberation movements as well as elements sharing similarities with Fascism, although it is a matter of debate whether Iraq was totalitarian at one point or another. The position of Iraq itself – with a population of Sunni and Shia Muslims, ethnic divisions between Arabs, Kurds, and others, and similar divisions – also straddles territory between Arabic Sunni populations to its west and Persian Shia populations to its east. The destruction of the Iraqi government by American and allied militaries in 2003 brought forward similar problems that arose with the Weimar Republic, as well as other countries: what new government should be put in place? Should members of the former regime be allowed to serve in government? Should the general population of the defeated country have input in the new constitution? Can an imposed constitution garner legitimacy from the local population? But the situation in Iraq also presented additional challenges, specifically how to deal with the religious and ethnic divides in the country, as well as how to handle the other types of social organizations (such as tribal affiliations) that played a substantial role in the nation. The end result was a great deal of instability, not only within Iraq but also outside of it. Iraq served as a "proving ground" of sorts for various totalitarian organizations, while also spawning new ones. These organizations and their members would then play a substantial role in the Syrian Civil War (2011–present). Once again, many of the ideas and some organizations were already in place. The writings of Sayyid Qutb were already influential, and the Muslim Brotherhood in one form or another had existed since 1928. Members of Al Qaeda – obviously already in existence before the Iraq War – also became active in the region, where they could spread both their ideology and their organizational forms to new populations. The combination of mass politics, instability, and various forms of Islamism set the stage for various types of totalitarianism (among other forms of rule).[20] The most notable result of this crisis is the rise of the Islamic State,[21] which made massive gains (as well as declaring itself a global caliphate) in 2014. Gerges describes the role of instability in the revival of ISIS,[22] which would likely have remained one of many disparate groups (or even just disgruntled individuals) were it not for the crisis created through the Iraq War.

Let's try to narrow down the similarities in these two examples. There are three traits that we can see as helping a totalitarian movement/organization gain strength and momentum. First, the breakdown of day-to-day life provides ample ground for totalitarianism to grow in popularity. If even basic activities become daunting tasks, people will be more receptive to radical ideas that bring about a solution. The most obvious example of such a breakdown would be warfare. Being in constant fear of artillery shells or snipers when walking down the street would make simple things (like going to the store) a life-and-death gamble. But other typical examples include situations where, among other things, extreme inflation is present. Many of you have probably seen a famous photograph from Germany during the Weimar Republic (1918–1933) where a few children are filling a wheelbarrow full of currency – millions worth of Deutschmarks – just to buy a loaf of bread. "Disruptive" is a mild term for situations where a person does not know if a loaf of bread will go from costing two dollars to $20,000 to $2 million in a period of a few weeks. Second, the collapse of previous forms of authority provides totalitarian parties/movements with an opportunity for taking on authority for themselves. When talking about the collapse of authority, I don't mean the complete absence of authority, such as the anarchy that arises when a government completely abdicates itself. Instead, this collapse refers to a "legitimacy crisis" (or, depending upon one's preference, a "legitimation crisis"[23]). Authority can, to an extent, maintain itself through pure force and coercion, but this type of rule is highly unstable and rather costly. A government (or a social institution) generally needs to be viewed as legitimate by a substantial part of the population if it is to remain functional or effective.[24]

Third, the sheer uncertainty about the future during a crisis situation can make totalitarian organizations seem much more attractive. This third point is important to consider, just as a matter of one's own experience. While none of us know what our future will hold, we usually make some broad (and generally safe) assumptions: that we will have a job, that we may move where we live (but to rather stable cities), that perhaps we'll get married and have children, and other things of that nature. A notable feature of these crisis points is that this sense of a broad, more-or-less-stable future tends to vanish. When even the continuation of one's own country is up in the air, it becomes monumentally difficult to think through one's own future. While a totalitarian movement sounds viciously unpleasant in normal times, the firm future the movement offers can be quite reassuring when the future appears at best uncertain and at worst an empty shell.

Conclusion

Ideas in the realm of theory need organization in the realm of practical action to influence politics, and totalitarian ideologies are no different. But unlike other types of political organizations, totalitarian parties and movements have some typical means of structuring themselves, and also some usual means by which they try to influence broader movements. Finally, and again in contrast to many other types of political organizations, totalitarian parties and groups must rely heavily upon crisis in order to gain control of a political system. In most cases, totalitarians fail at gaining power or holding onto it for very long. Thankfully, totalitarian regimes have been a rare occurrence in history thus far. But, these regimes have existed, so we will now turn to how totalitarianism governs.

Summing Up

- To gain any influence, totalitarian ideas require a movement, and especially some form of organization.
- Many totalitarian groups will arrange themselves in a "vanguard party" form of organization.
- It is rare for a totalitarian organization to gain full power on its own. It usually attaches itself to some broader social/political movement and seeks to dominate it.
- Historically, totalitarian parties/movements need some type of crisis to exist in order to gain political power.

Suggested Reading

As with ideologies, most analyses of totalitarian movements and organizations focus on specific ones, rather than as a general phenomenon. Books that do focus on totalitarian movements more generally tend to focus on the psychology of movement members and can be a bit "impressionistic," for lack of a better word. Even so, these examinations can be useful. The best work of this type for introductory readers is probably Hoffer (1951). While focused on terrorist (rather than specifically totalitarian) organizations, a good source is Silke (2019), while a more concise (if somewhat dated) rough-and-ready reference is Ashley (2011). A greater selection exists when turning to specific totalitarian movements and/or groups. Excellent sources on Communist and Marxist-based movements include Brown (2009) and Service (2007), while McLellan (2007) gives a good sense of some of the totalitarian and non-totalitarian variants that arise after Marx's death. When looking to nationalist (especially Fascist) movements, the best source by far is Payne (1995), while Sternhell (1994) gives an interesting overview and Schnapp (2000) provides some helpful primary texts. For racialist movements, Payne (1995) also provides a good overview, which can be helpfully supplemented by some of the primary sources in Griffin (1995). A fully satisfying overview of Islamist movements still awaits to be written, but helpful sources include Juergensmeyer (2003), Rinehart (2013), and Hegghammer (2017), among others. While an older study, Mitchell (1969)'s book on the early Muslim Brotherhood is an excellent read.

Notes

1. Lenin (1969[1902]).
2. Obviously, there are significantly more rigorous and technical definitions of "mass politics," but we do not need such specification here.
3. See Kendall and Carey (1995).
4. "a free co-operative association of peasants which periodically distributed the agricultural land to be tilled, and whose decisions bound all its members" (Chamberlain 2007: 122).
5. My thanks to Justin Gray for these observations on mass involvement in ancient politics.
6. For a most useful discussion on changes in the state, see Strayer (1970).
7. Perhaps the most famous discussion of this issue is in Michels (1962).
8. Azzam (2008): 140.
9. For greater discussion on vanguard parties, see Unger (1974); Gray (2020).
10. Emphasis in original. Lenin (1969[1902]): 107.
11. A good source is Schumann (2009).
12. Della Porta and Diani (2006): 20.
13. We can use some of the language from political science (focused on interest groups) for this distinction. People who belong to a specific organization (vanguard party or otherwise) would be "actual members" of the movement (meaning that they are constantly, consistently, and predominantly focused on the movement's advancement), while people who are somewhat interested in the movement will participate in protests, boycotts, or other activities, and would be "potential members," with "actual members" often trying to bring these "potential members" in to an organization as "actual members."
14. Discussions of charisma usually focus on the work of the influential sociologist Max Weber. For a good rundown on this particular topic, see Baehr (2008).
15. While in a very different context, a humorist on Twitter has summed up the process of entryism rather well: "1) Identify a respected institution. 2) kill it. 3) gut it. 4) wear its carcass as a skin suit, while demanding respect" (Burge 2015).
16. Tackett (2015): 63.
17. For a good discussion of such blindness, specifically dealing with Communist/Marxist regimes, see Hollander (1998).
18. For a very interesting analysis of crisis and extremism, see Midlarsky (2011).
19. For those inclined to read interesting, if somewhat archaic, medical texts on this topic, see Lloyd (1983).
20. See Hamid (2014).
21. Also known as the Islamic State of Iraq and the Levant (ISIL), the Islamic State of Iraq and Syria (ISIS), and as Daesh.
22. Gerges (2016): 98–143.
23. Habermas (1973).
24. To illustrate the difference between authority with legitimacy versus authority through sheer force, let's use a silly example. Imagine that we

are in a classroom, and I am lecturing to you. Halfway through class, two men wearing suits and carrying pistols come in to the room, saying, "Professor Gray, we are from the Brazos County Sheriff's Department. We have a warrant for your arrest, on the charge of illegal trash burning in the county." They show me their badges and the arrest warrant. I go with them willingly to the patrol car, even if the officers are a little incompetent (they don't fasten my handcuffs, they drop their car keys, they keep looking into the distance without watching me). I think they have made a mistake, but I recognize that they are legitimate officers of the law who (as far as I can tell) have followed the proper, legitimate procedures for this arrest. Compare this to another situation: same lecture, same suits, same weapons, same incompetence on the officers' parts, but the "authority" is different. The men come in and say, "Professor Gray, we are from the Security Office of the Microsoft Corporation. In Section 493, Subsection 72, Paragraph 5 of the user agreement for Windows 10 – and which you clicked 'I accept' to the terms – requires that you provide three gallons of blood to Microsoft each financial quarter. You have not. Therefore, on the authority of a detention warrant from Microsoft, we are taking you to our company incarceration center in Seattle." I will probably go with them initially, but not as the result of my recognition of them as legitimate, but instead because I don't want to be shot. But if they fumble their keys or are staring into the distance, I will run as fast as I can. As soon as the immediate coercion is not there, I will do everything in my power to get away. If an authority is recognized as legitimate, it significantly decreases the amount of *actual* coercion or force it needs to use.

Bibliography

Ashley, Paul. 2011. *The Complete Encyclopedia of Terrorist Organizations*. Philadelphia: Casemate.

Azzam, Abdallah. 2008. "The Solid Base (Excerpts)." In Gilles Kepel and Jean-Pierre Milelli (eds.), *Al-Qaeda in Its Own Words*. Pascale Ghazaleh, trans. Cambridge: Belknap Press, pp. 140–143.

Baehr, Peter. 2008. *Caesarism, Charisma, and Fate: Historical Sources and Modern Resonances in the Work of Max Weber*. New Brunswick: Transaction Publishers.

Brown, Archie. 2009. *The Rise and Fall of Communism*. New York: Ecco.

Burge, David [iowahawk]. 2015 (November 10). "1. Identify a Respected Institution. 2. Kill It. 3. Gut It. 4. Wear Its Carcass as a Skin Suit, While Demanding Respect. #lefties." [tweet]. Retrieved from: https://twitter.com/iowahawkblog/status/664089892599631872.

Chamberlain, Lesley. 2007. *Motherland: A Philosophical History of Russia*. New York: Overlook/Rookery.

Della Porta, Donatella, and Mario Diani. 2006. *Social Movements: An Introduction*. Second Edition. Malden, MA: Blackwell Publishing.

Gerges, Fawaz A. 2016. *ISIS: A History*. Princeton: Princeton University Press.

Gray, Phillip W. 2020. *Vanguardism: Ideology and Organization in Totalitarian Politics*. New York: Routledge.

Griffin, Roger (ed.). 1995. *Fascism*. Oxford: Oxford University Press.

Habermas, Jürgen. 1973. *Legitimation Crisis*. Cambridge: MIT Press.

Hamid, Shadi. 2014. *Temptations of Power: Islamists and Illiberal Democracy in a New Middle East*. Oxford: Oxford University Press.

Hegghammer, Thomas (ed.). 2017. *Jihadi Culture: The Art and Social Practices of Militant Islamists*. Cambridge: Cambridge University Press.

Hoffer, Eric. 1951. *The True Believer: Thoughts on the Nature of Mass Movements*. New York: Harper Perennial.

Hollander, Paul. 1998. *Political Pilgrims: Western Intellectuals in Search of the Good Society*. Fourth Edition. New Brunswick: Transaction Publishers.

Juergensmeyer, Mark. 2003. *Terror in the Mind of God: The Global Rise of Religious Violence*. Berkeley: University of California Press.

Kendall, Willmoore, and George W. Carey. 1995. *The Basic Symbols of the American Political Tradition*. Washington, DC: Catholic University of America Press.

Lenin, V. I. 1969[1902]. *What Is To Be Done? Burning Questions of Our Movement*. New York: International Publishers.

Lloyd, G. E. R., ed. 1983. *Hippocratic Writings*. New York: Penguin Books.

McLellan, David. 2007. *Marxism after Marx*. Fourth Edition. New York: Palgrave Macmillan.

Michels, Robert. 1962. *Political Parties: A Sociological Study of the Oligarchical Tendencies of Modern Democracy*. Eden and Cedar Paul, trans. New York: Free Press.

Midlarsky, Manus I. 2011. *Origins of Political Extremism: Mass Violence in the Twentieth Century*. Cambridge: Cambridge University Press.

Mitchell, Richard P. 1969. *The Society of Muslim Brothers*. Oxford: Oxford University Press.

Payne, Stanley G. 1995. *A History of Fascism, 1914–1945*. Madison: University of Wisconsin Press.

Rinehart, Christine Sixta. 2013. *Volatile Social Movements and the Origins of Terrorism: The Radicalization of Change*. Lanham: Lexington Books.

Schnapp, Jeffrey T. (ed.). 2000. *Primer of Italian Fascism*. Lincoln, NE: University of Nebraska.

Schumann, Dirk. 2009. *Political Violence in the Weimar Republic, 1918–1933: Fight for the Streets and Fear of Civil War*. Thomas Dunlap, trans. New York: Berghahn Books.

Service, Robert. 2007. *Comrades: A History of World Communism*. Cambridge: Harvard University Press.

Silke, Andrew (ed.). 2019. *Routledge Handbook of Terrorism and Counterterrorism*. London: Routledge.

Sternhell, Zeev. 1994. *The Birth of Fascist Ideology: From Cultural Rebellion to Political Revolution*. David Maisel, trans. Princeton: Princeton University Press.

Strayer, Joseph R. 1970. *On the Medieval Origins of the Modern State*. Princeton: Princeton University Press.

Tackett, Timothy. 2015. *The Coming of the Terror in the French Revolution*. Cambridge: Belknap Press.

Unger, Aryeh L. 1974. *The Totalitarian Party: Party and People in Nazi Germany and Soviet Russia*. Cambridge: Cambridge University Press.

REGIME
How Totalitarianism Governs

Ideology and movement/party are central parts of totalitarianism. But when most people think about totalitarianism, the first things that come to their minds are totalitarian governments, be they historical regimes or fictional representations of totalitarianism as dystopian futures. In such novels, however, we see totalitarian government in its solid, well-established form. Ladies are in breeding gowns, men are goosestepping around in fancy uniforms, Big Brother's face is already omnipresent everywhere, and there is no real sense in any of these places that a realistic threat to the government exists. But is this how it goes in reality? One day, a society is unstable and suffering internal divisions, but the next day everyone "loves Big Brother very much," takes their Soma, and goes along as cogs in a totalitarian system? Not quite.

Let's look at what happens when a totalitarian organization actually gains power. Rather than columns of stormtroopers marching down the streets before terrified citizens, one often finds much of the population welcoming the new system. Some of the population agrees with the totalitarian movement's aims and ideas, at least broadly. The trade unionist in Russia might think the Bolsheviks are a bit "out there," but generally on the "Right Side of History;" the German nationalist might find Nazi racialism rather odd, but that it "more or less" leans in the correct direction. These people – as well as many observers in other countries – tend to believe that the responsibilities of governance will "calm down" the totalitarian leaders and make them more "reasonable." This is generally an incorrect assumption, to put it mildly. But, for most people in a country, welcoming the new system likely reflects the population's general indifference (at

DOI: 10.4324/9781003254232-4

best) to the previous system and its instability, corruptions, and whatever else. In effect, these people believe that things couldn't possibly get worse than they already are, only to discover too late that things could get much worse indeed.[1]

There are six parts to this chapter. First, we will discuss totalitarian governments as a "regime-type," or a "family" of states that share fundamental similarities. The second part will talk about how these regimes try to implement the totalism at the foundation of their ideologies. In the third part, we talk about some of the day-to-day life experiences of people within totalitarian regimes, which could range from utterly horrific to being viewed as a wonderful change. Both the second and third parts will also address the roles of propaganda and surveillance within totalitarian states. Fourth, we will discuss the role of terror within these types of governments. The fifth part will talk about the centrality of killing in most totalitarian regimes. Sixth, we will talk about life after totalitarianism and post-totalitarian states. So, to begin, let's look at regime types.

Totalitarianism as Regime Type

Before going over specific traits within totalitarian governments, we should note what we mean by "regime type." We tangentially noted the notion of "regime" in Chapter 1, but now is the time to flesh out this idea a little more. In disciplines like political science, a "regime type" refers to a grouping of government systems that share certain fundamental similarities, and these shared traits can also distinguish one grouping of governments from other such groupings. There are various qualities that are used for regime type, which can include:

- Who "counts" as a citizen?
- How are leaders chosen?
- Are there separations of power within the government?
- Are there certain rights/protections that are recognized? And, if so, how they are recognized?
- What kinds of restrictions exist on government?

Much of this can be determined by looking at the laws and regulations of a country. And, indeed, the ancient Greek philosopher Aristotle had various students collect this type of information in the late 300s BC/BCE, but one needs to also be aware of the practical reality of a system as well. The Soviet Union presents an excellent example of the dissonance between written laws/constitutions compared to the "on the ground" reality. The Soviet Union's Constitution of 1936 was a quite beautiful document, including protections for religion, speech, assembly and association, and numerous other things. But note that it was put in place in 1936, starting the same year as what is usually called the "Great Purge," usually considered one of the most totalitarian and vicious periods of Stalin's rule. A government may have a very pretty constitution and praiseworthy laws, but if they are not enforced or followed, what might appear to be a "democratic" system may be something rather different.

"Regime type," in this sense, would be like the types of categorizations you would find in biology, such as those that distinguish the class of mammals ("Mammalia") from the class of birds ("Aves"). While there are major differences between humans, dolphins, and badgers, they share fundamental characteristics among themselves, and these characteristics distinguish them from pigeons, penguins, and falcons. The most basic regime type one frequently hears about today is the democratic regime type, contrasted with non-democracies, although this breakdown leaves "non-democracies" rather unspecified (rather akin to a simple distinction of mammals and "non-mammals," although one should question the type of similarities between a penguin, a starfish, and an earthworm).

As a comparison, we often talk about "democracy" as a regime type. "Regime type" is a broad category that contains a great deal of internal diversity. The political systems of the United States, Sweden, and South Korea are all categorized as part of the "democratic" regime type, but none of these systems are exactly alike one another. Obviously, the sundry types of governments that are usually called "democracies" have notable variations between them. For instance, while both the United States and the United Kingdom are called democracies, one of them is a parliamentary system with legally recognized hereditary positions in government, while the other is a presidential system with no legally mandated hereditary positions. The United Kingdom has an "unwritten constitution" that arises from centuries of laws, practices, and customs, while the United States has a written constitution. But even with these many – and often not insignificant – differences, we can understand that these governments share some underlying, foundational similarities. A major commonality is that all these systems have elections for public office, and that most citizens can vote. Additionally, these governments exhibit some level of separation between government powers (the most notable being the comparative independence of the courts from executive or legislative pressure), recognize certain types of rights of citizens, and generally hold that public officials' actions must relate to some specific, written-down law or regulation. To go back to our biology example, we might say these distinctions are like species categorizations. Just as rabbits and badgers are members of the Mammalia class but belong to different families ("Leporidae" and "Mustelidae," respectively), so too are the United States and the United Kingdom both democracies – but they are from different "families" (or "species," or whatever other classificatory language you prefer) of democracy. Likewise, we often make comparable distinctions with dictatorships. They may vary in type (military dictatorships, hereditary dictatorships, populist dictatorships), but they also share important elements that relate each of them to the "regime type" of dictatorship. Theoretically, at least, one could categorize almost any government system into these regime-type families.

So, too, with totalitarian governments. While there are obvious and major differences between, for instance, Nazi Germany and the People's Republic of China under Mao, they also share fundamental similarities that would place them in the same "family" as the totalitarian regime type. The discussions on ideology and movements in Chapters 2 and 3 have already pointed out some of these overlapping elements, and these also show themselves in totalitarian governments and states. A key aspect of the totalitarian regime type would be "totalistic party rule." But here, we have to be specific. There are many countries that are one-party states. Indeed, one can even find one-party rule in various regions and/or cities within democracies (for instance, the American cities of Chicago and Atlanta have been under the continuous control of the Democratic Party since 1931 and 1879, respectively). While this type of continuous one-party rule isn't generally healthy in a democracy, and may reflect issues of corruption and/or dysfunction in these localities, they remain just that – dysfunctions, rather than fundamental structures. Totalitarian one-party states are fundamentally different. In effect, the party is the actual ruling institution in the country, even if the government apparatus (or at least parts of it) is technically separate from the party. If we look at a Communist system, even if the chairperson of the party's main ruling committee isn't technically a public official – in other words, s/he doesn't hold the position of president, premier, legislator, or the like – the chairperson is actually the person who truly rules the country. The chairperson (in conjunction with the main party committee) is the one who sets down the policies that will be implemented by the government. Moreover, the party is the actual "backbone" of the government. Usually, people cannot serve in government unless they belong to the party and will lose their government position if they are expelled from the party (or are no longer members "in good standing"). Throughout the government itself, especially within the bureaucracy, there is a proliferation of political "commissars," populated by party members whose job it is to "supervise" and "educate" members of the government (public administrators, soldiers in the military, and elsewhere) in the governing ideology, as well as to act as a monitor against anti-ideology thoughts or organizations among the people the commissars "supervise." The totalitarian government depends upon these types of party extensions within the political system itself, and usually also tries to similarly extend itself into the various social systems in the country, like schools, small associations, clubs, and even families. Indeed, the totalitarian system could not continue to function without this party expansion, and this is true across totalitarian systems (Communist or otherwise). If the Democratic Party in the United States should vanish tomorrow, it would cause some upheaval (and certainly a great deal of confusion), but the government of the city of Chicago would still exist and could still function without the Democrats. In contrast, if the Chinese Communist Party ceased to exist in the city of Guangzhou, the governing system would completely collapse, as the governmental system requires the party in order to function.

There can be some variation in the structure of totalistic party rule, of course, and the variations are generally the result of historical influences on particular types of totalitarian movements. For instance, Communist states usually have a central "political committee" or "political bureau" (often shortened to Politburo) that is the highest authority in the country, although these can end up under the control of one dominant figure (Stalin and Mao being the most famous examples). Communist party-states often have a proliferation of committees that construct policies for the government, such as aforementioned "political bureau," as well as groups like the "organizational bureau," that are often referred to through acronyms, like "Politburo" or "Orgburo." Moreover, in larger Communist party-states, there are usually regional party committees and city party committees (for larger or more important urban areas). The large numbers of committees do not exist just to give party members employment (although that does play a bit of a role). Instead, these committees act to solidify party control over government, as well as to ensure party coordination and hierarchy.[2] Think of the example of Patton from Chapter 3. Just as a movement needs multiple units and leaders to be successful, a party that now runs the government needs even more organizational "meshing" in order to maintain its position and ensure that no part of the government (or the party) gets "out of line," be it ideologically, in terms of implementation, or in trying to overtake other parts of the government/party.

There are other structures that totalitarian party-states use to control the government. Many other totalitarian systems follow a notion of the "leadership principle" (or "*Führerprinzip*"), meaning that the key role of decision-maker is placed upon the person of the leader more than being based on specific legal specifications. In other words, one could say that position/office is more important than process/legality in a "leadership principle" totalitarian system. Mussolini and Hitler are the biggest examples of this type, but we need to avoid falling into simplistic notions. In these systems, the "leadership principle" applies most readily and completely to the top leader – to the *Duce* of Italy or the *Führer* of Germany – but it also applies to leaders further down the hierarchy, particularly as regards party leaders. Organizationally, this makes sense. Even if the highest leaders were as hard-working and all-wise as their hagiographers made them out to be, one person could not handle all of the necessary decisions within even a middle-sized town, much less for a whole country. As such, the "leadership principle" applies in a way that is somewhat similar to the party committees mentioned earlier, but instead of it being run by a group of party members, it is headed by one person. Probably the best comparison to this structure would be how leadership and hierarchy works in a military (lieutenants under captains under majors under colonels, and so forth). There are other differences as well, however. Rather than "seeping into" all aspects of government in the manner of the committees mentioned earlier, "leadership principle" systems tend to make "parallel institutions." In other words, the party will have its own regional or organization-specific party organs, which then oversee and/or dictate to the actual government officers.[3] Other differences also exist between totalitarian party-governments, such as comparative levels of centralization, but we can leave them to the side.

Another core regime-type trait for totalitarian states is the basis for its form of legitimacy. Back in Chapter 3, we talked about legitimacy in relation to crisis, and how crises can lessen the legitimacy of a country that a totalitarian party wishes to control. But now, we will consider legitimacy from the other side: what legitimacy means for an established government (and particularly, for a totalitarian government). As noted in that earlier discussion, a government needs legitimacy to enforce its will since simple coercion and force can be hard to maintain for extended periods of time. A government that keeps its power solely through ongoing pressure and force would soon run into numerous problems. The sheer costs (in money and personnel) would be overwhelming, and any even slight lessening of coercion from the government would likely result in much of the population revolting. Obviously, numerous governments are far from shy about using force to ensure their positions. But even for these governments, there needs to be something else – some claim to being the "true" government, some customary ties that maintain order, even some impression of inevitability of rule – that will cause the population to recognize (even if grudgingly) the government's authority. For instance, democracies gain legitimacy as representing "the consent of the governed," meaning that the governing system is acceptable – and that people should be loyal to the government – because it is the population itself, through its representatives, where power actually resides in the government. If it should arise that a significant part of the citizenry does not believe it is "consenting" to democracy, such as the belief that government isn't responsive or that corruption has put into question democratic accountability, then a democracy will have to make major reforms or use a significant level of coercion to curb a possible revolt.

Within totalitarian governments, their legitimacy primarily comes from three sources (although, in any specific instance, there may be other, additional sources that are used). First is the totalitarian ideology, in that it reflects the "true reality" of the world. Rather than being based on traditions and customs, or some notion of the "consent of the governed," legitimacy arises from knowing the direction of History and its movement toward a "higher" form of society. The ideology provides the "framework" and "worldview" in which this type of legitimacy can function. A modern democratic system (for instance) often has the underlying "worldview" that each individual has a certain level of reason and holds a certain number of rights, so the governing system is a means of recognizing and protecting these rights among different people. The ideology of totalitarian regimes, on the other hand, emphasize the notion of History and its implications for reality. If History is *by necessity* moving toward full egalitarianism or toward direct rule by God, then legitimacy arises from moving in the direction of History, regardless of what any one person (or even all people) would happen to prefer at a given time. For the totalitarian regime's ideology, focusing upon the "consent of the governed" would be as nonsensical as taking a vote on whether gravity will still function. While the vast majority might vote to revoke gravity (because flying around is awesome), reality – or at least the totalitarian ideology's conception of reality – has the final word. In a sense, this type of legitimacy is "the Right Side of History" on steroids. The second source of legitimacy is that the party accurately understands the direction and dynamics of History and can therefore lead others toward the "New Society." Whether the idea is that the government will guide the "glorious revolution" toward the "classless society," that the government will build the new "master race," or some other notion, the "legitimating" idea is that the government is on the side of History and is helping move society along to its inevitable and "higher" form of organization. If the ideology is true (and, as we will discuss later, totalitarian regimes put major effort into getting the population to believe its ideas), then it makes logical sense that the people who know the "science" of it should be in charge of governing. Just as a person with a tumor would really prefer treatment from a highly competent surgeon, so too should a society want its far-seeing "vanguard" to guide the country toward its "better" and "healthy" condition. Third, and particularly important, is that the party does not have power from itself, like an enlightened group of philosopher-kings, but rather has its power through the central importance of the "world-historic" population in the country. This world-historic population could be the majority of people in the country (such as Italians for Mussolini's Fascists), but they might be a minority as well (for instance, industrial workers in Russia for the Communists or "true Muslims" in the territory of the Islamic State). But remember, this type of legitimacy is *not* based on "consent of the governed," whether in reality or even in theory. As mentioned earlier, the democratic notion of consent operates within a certain "worldview" that holds certain beliefs about the nature of human beings (such as reason and rights) and their interactions in collective groups. It is in this "worldview" that democracy, at least at a theoretical level, gains its legitimacy. Totalitarian regimes do not share this "worldview," as is obvious, but this also applies to the "world-historic" population. While History "moves" through this population, it is not the result of the "world-historic" population's consent or choice, any more than cesium "chooses" or "consents" to explosively react when exposed to water. There is a strong under-current of determinism within most totalitarian ideologies. Human acts do matter in making social revolution, totalitarian regimes, and the sought after "New Society," but they operate within a system of reality that largely acts by necessity, just like the cause-and-effect in chemistry or other physical sciences.

Finally, the totalitarian regime type includes the lack of limiting principle upon the totalitarian party-state. Chapter 2 briefly mentioned how "totalism" could also be called a "lack of limiting principle," but one can have greater clarity on the meaning of this phrase when looking at totalitarian regimes. A limiting principle would be some norm (it can be written into law, but it can also be an informal custom), fundamental restriction, or "side-restraint" that bars a government from acting in some ways. The most obvious example of such a limit would be the Bill of Rights in the United States Constitution. With it, the government is barred from blocking the freedom of speech, is barred from arresting people without due process, and so forth. Beyond just the Constitution, however, there are other norms related to these ideas. An example of such an informal norm would be that the government should not to attempt to force religious organizations to change their internal theologies, such as using anti-discrimination law to coerce the Catholic Church into having women priests, as an example. But this type of limiting principle isn't only a trait of modern democracies. Traditional monarchies also had limiting principles. While the king, theoretically, was not bound by the law, he was bound by tradition, certain older traditions, and certain types of feudal contracts. Even military dictatorships, which would also seem to lack any limits, have some limiting principles. At the most basic level, the continued maintenance of the military's internal hierarchy (lieutenants do not countermand the orders of majors) creates a certain limiting function. Additionally, these other types of regimes also often have limitations on what spheres of life they will attempt to control. Once again, religion tends to be the biggest example, as one can see in the conflicts between Church and State in Western European history. A unique trait of the totalitarian regime type, separate from other types, is its lack of limiting principle. There is no aspect of life – political, social, economic, personal – that is outside the sphere of the government's control and influence. Obviously, no totalitarian government has ever managed to gain such control, and, in practice, many of them had temporary limits.[4] But, in a sense, this is similar to noting that it is a rare democratic government that can really say it has the full-throated "consent of the governed." Within totalitarian ideology, and as advanced within totalitarian regimes, there is no area of life that is outside the reach of "History," and thus outside the reach of the government. As such, there is no "limiting principle" to the government itself. Any and all parts of life *must* be under the control of the regime, even if the totalitarian regime is not explicitly pushing for control in a given sphere of life at any specific time.

"Everything in the State, Nothing Outside the State, Nothing Against the State"

As a regime, totalitarianism attempts to control, or at least influence, every element of human interaction. As the ideology is totalistic, so too must the society be totalistic. For some parts of society, this control is rather explicit. All political parties (or even general social groups) are illegal except for ones directed by the government/party, criticizing the totalitarian ideology will lead to various types of punishments (loss of job, loss of house, loss of freedom, loss of life), and the main foundation for any part of society's legitimacy is the totalitarian ideology/system (the factory acts as the embryonic instance of the "classless society," the family serves as the perpetuator of the "Master Race," and so forth). In other areas, the control or influence is more implicit and feared, such as in the worry that a neighbor or coworker might be an informant for the secret police, waiting to report you for telling an "incorrect" joke or saying something negative about the leadership. The overall impression is that someone is always watching you, everywhere. Or perhaps it might be better to say some*thing* is watching. The party and the state take on an almost omniscient status in the minds of much of the population.

But doesn't such a focus on government power seem to undermine the totalitarian party's own ideology? As noted in Chapter 2, almost all totalitarian ideologies view something other than politics as the main "driving force" of History. Pride of place goes to economics, biology, culture, God, or some other thing. For ideological systems that view politics as secondary and derivative, why would they place such importance on government taking control of everything once in power? Leaving aside the (not incorrect but a bit too shallow) view that people who gain political power will often find themselves conveniently more inclined toward increasing that power, there are two major reasons. First and foremost, the idea of "false consciousness" is important. Although the totalitarian party now has power, there is a sense that the totalitarians are still operating at a significant disadvantage. The vast majority of the country, including the "world-historic" population, were born and raised under the previous system, which means the majority grew up following the rules of the previous system, internalizing the old system's norms, and indeed even thinking the way the previous system indoctrinated them to think. For most of these totalitarian governments, there is a sense that political power must be used strongly, broadly, and deeply across all of society to "fight back" against the past. While not the best comparison, it is somewhat equivalent to the notion of "deprogramming" someone who has been involved in a cult of one form or another. The difference here is that the old system is the "cult" and it is almost the whole of society that is being "deprogrammed." A second reason, partially related to the first, deals with the totalitarian notion of "Enemies." In their view, just as the "Enemy" populations used all of the resources of society to stymie and crush the "forward progress" of History, so too should the totalitarian regime destroy those "counter-revolutionaries" who would try to stop the forward momentum of the regime. We will talk more later about the role of "Enemies" in totalitarian governments. With these two factors, totalitarian governments consistently view themselves as "underdogs" fighting off the relics of the past as well as Enemies in the present. Even if the government has something like 95% control over the society, it will still not be enough. As the vanguard party itself knows from its own experience, a small population can end up making huge advances. But even if the totalitarian government should garner complete and total power over everything in the state – even the very minds of the population – it still would not be enough. As long as there are governments or powers outside of it (such as other nations with different ideologies and rulers), the totalitarians will perceive themselves as fighting an uphill battle.

The aim of total control goes far beyond strong-arm methods and the fear of surveillance, although they often work in conjunction with such tactics. The totalitarian regime pushes for complete allegiance to the "mass line" or toward *Gleichschaltung*. No part of life can be isolated from the regime's ideology and goals, even if these aspects of living appear to have little or no connection with politics. In effect, the totalitarian regime "shifts" all of life to reflect, legitimize, and emphasize the ruling ideology. Education and culture are central examples of this expansion into all aspects of life.[5] All type of governments – at least as far as they are able – seek to control the education of the young, as the perpetuation of the system depends upon each new generation "buying into" it. But here, again, is the issue of a limiting principle. Most of these governments focus specifically on the government system (extolling how democracy is the best system, or how the "Divine Right of Kings" can be found in the Bible, for instance), and often on putting the best impression on the government's history, but will often engage less with other areas. While history and civics should reenforce the government's legitimacy, there is no "democratic chemistry" or "monarchist mathematics," for instance.

For totalitarian regimes, on the other hand, the ideology enters into every aspect of education and culture, be it through commending the regime and ideology or through condemning ideas and groups that are "Enemies." The sheer level of propaganda – understood as "propagating" ideology in any possible venue – is a clear element in totalitarian societies. Posters, loudspeaker messages, and various other signs and texts crowd out all other types of dialogue and styles of thinking in a such a society (as much as possible, at any rate). Among many examples, propaganda includes:

- Mandatory education on "dialectic materialism" in Communist societies or on eugenics in a Nazi state, which can involve full-on courses on the topic in secondary schools and colleges, but also more subtle "morality tales" and children's stories for primary schools.
- Mass media reports, posters, and texts regarding "everyday heroes" of the totalitarian regime, such as Alexei Stakhanov,[6] or "martyrs" of the ideology, such as Horst Wessel.[7]
- Ubiquitous sloganeering (on mass media, in mass organized "rallies," and elsewhere) that constantly hammers certain themes, points, or ideas. The slogans on eliminating the "Four Olds" and advancing the "Four News" during the Cultural Revolution in Communist China would be a key example.[8]
- Media representations (often visual media of some type) of the "Enemy," which can vary from a single person (such as the focus on Trotsky in Stalin's Soviet Union) to whole populations (such as the "kulaks" in the Soviet Union or Jews in Nazi Germany) as well as other nations. Typically, the Enemy is presented as subhuman and as "vermin," but also insidiously sneaking its way into the "good" totalitarian society (with the Enemy compared to spiders, an octopus, viruses, or the like).

The aim is to dominate the "battlespace" of ideas and life. If every part of life is connected with the regime, with what the totalitarian state prefers being praised and what it dislikes being condemned, the intention is to make thinking and perceiving in other ways difficult for those living in these countries. Moreover, the intention is for this type of propaganda to be "self-perpetuating," for lack of a better word. As humans are social beings, a substantial part of the population will take in this propaganda as the truth, as the perhaps unconscious impression will be that "everyone else believes this is true, so I should as well." In its more extreme forms, a small number of instigators can mobilize a large part of the population to proclaim the "truth" of the regime against "Enemies." The dreaded struggle sessions in Communist China during the Cultural Revolution are good examples, and one can see similar struggle session tactics used in other types of totalitarian states and organizations.

Finally, associations between people in a totalitarian state also must reflect the ideology and policies of the regime. Once again, Lenin provides the early example of this framework. Regarding trade unions, Lenin argued that they should agitate for change under capitalist systems; but once the "vanguard of the proletariat" was in control of government, the purpose of trade unions was to act as a "transmission belt" for ensuring the spread of the ideology and loyalty to the regime. All things being equal, all types of independent, unconnected associations of people must be barred in a totalitarian state and subsumed under the control of the regime itself. Although totalitarian regimes cannot often go that far (for instance, in lacking the ability to eliminate the family, or many of these states lacking the power to completely destroy religious organizations), they will try to expand this power as much as possible. So, what would this "look like" in practice? If someone wants to have a sewing club in Stalin's Soviet Union, it must align with the Communist Party (or indeed, even be a subsidiary part of it), and must maintain the "correct" view on capitalist exploitation of textile workers. If someone wants to have a chess club in Nazi Germany, it must hold the "correct" views on Jewish influence in games. Do little sewing clubs have any real connection to international economic dynamics? Do chess clubs need any position on the "Jewish Question"? A hallmark of a totalitarian regime is to answer "yes." No association is too small, no person too socially insignificant that they can be spared the obligation to hold the "correct" views and exhibit proper "enthusiasm" for the regime and its goals. This saturation of the ideology into all parts of society plays a significant role in what life is like under totalitarianism.

Living in the Totalitarian State

As mentioned at the start of this chapter, most of us (thankfully) only have a literary sense of life in a totalitarian regime, be it from novels we've read in school, movies we've seen, and so forth. Usually, we envision life as a dark dystopia, epitomized by constant fear. And, indeed, fear and terror play a sizeable role in the totalitarian state, which we will discuss in the following. But a totalitarian state – especially one that manages to exist for longer than a few weeks or months – cannot *only* rely on fear. It also needs a large part of the population to passively, and even actively, assist it. That doesn't mean that fear plays no role, of course. Even in what are viewed as the most free and democratic societies, fear plays a role in governance. When they are getting close to tax-day each year on 15 April, a wide variety of American citizens will have a palpable awareness and fear of the Internal Revenue Service, for instance. While a government cannot solely maintain itself on force and fear, it is also true that governments require some level of coercion and fear to operate, even if the system aims to be just and/or free. Totalitarian regimes obviously put more emphasis on the fear/force elements, but must also rely on passive acceptance (at least) from a sizeable part of the population. The saturation of society with the ideology aims to increase acceptance by the population, and indeed to move it beyond passive acceptance toward full-throated support. As noted earlier, a key purpose for the extensive propaganda in totalitarianism is to make acceptance of the ideology (and regime) "self-perpetuating" in society. It may be disconcerting to realize, but historically, this mix of saturation, fear, force, and propaganda has worked strikingly well in increasing popular acceptance and support for many unpleasant totalitarian regimes.

This level of popular acceptance tends to be overlooked for a variety of reasons. One key reason is simply that no one wants to be on the losing side, especially when that losing side was involved in quite a few atrocities. In terms of popular movies, memoirs, and the like, it is a rather small number of people who, for instance, acted as informants in Nazi Germany or Stalinist Russia who would want to advertise their activities in either of these regimes. Even if these former informants had no chance of being criminally prosecuted (after the end of the totalitarian government), such confessions would make them pariahs. Instead, people who may have been supportive of totalitarian regimes at the time would be more inclined to reframe their activities (not only when talking to others, but even when thinking about themselves) as forms of "hidden" resistance under impossible circumstances. One can see this even in places that were not purely totalitarian. It is an old joke that the French Resistance was a rather small group until the Nazis were repelled by Allied forces. Then, suddenly, a large number of people were "actually" part of the Resistance after the fact. There certainly are a significant number of people in totalitarian systems who do not support them, and who act in ways (often quite limited, as there is little else that can be done) to resist them, but it would be erroneous to think these people make up an overwhelming majority.

Another reason is harder to describe. For many people and societies, we would prefer to think that totalitarian regimes cannot possibly be rational; that they must be based on irrationality, hatred, easy scapegoating, fear, and similar non-rational foundations. The result is that we tend to look at those living in these societies (with the exceptions of those in leadership positions or directly involved in vicious acts) as not really acting in a fully rational way. In a sense, we *don't want to believe* that a sizeable amount of a population could view these regimes as rational, just, and moral. While that might speak well to our views of our fellow human beings, it does rather limit our ability to consider what everyday life is like in such a society. Within its own worldview, totalitarian ideologies and regimes can be highly rational (even if not necessarily reasonable), and thus the passive acceptance (or more) from the population is not irrational. People can be rationally evil, even in large numbers. The discussion so far may sound like an attempt to excuse or rationalize the actions of people in totalitarian states. It is not meant to be so. But it is meant to remind us that it is rather easy to believe that "of course" it would be obvious how evil, demented, and/or insane a regime might be when we are living decades after the regime was destroyed and its crimes a matter of common knowledge. It is easy to judge in hindsight, and it's easy to imagine ourselves as heroes in situations we have blessedly been spared from.

So, how would the typical day go for an average person in a totalitarian regime? In some ways, life would continue as normal. People would still go to work, romantic relationships would still form, children would be born, and the aged would pass away. While the "New Society" might be "just around the corner," according to the regime's propaganda, much of society remains as one would expect in any other place. But the mental framework of day-to-day life proceeds rather differently, which then puts a very different sheen upon one's "normal" activities. The way a "normal day" proceeds in totalitarian regimes often depends heavily on how long, and how strongly, the government has control over the country. In the early stages of the regime, especially if the totalitarian government has few obstacles, many parts of society take on an almost experimental feeling. The early Soviet Union, for instance, had various parts of the regime trying out "new ways of living" in the "New Society."[9] However, as time goes on, the Party's power solidifies and the typical needs of any country become more pressing, so the more typical parts of life come to the forefront again: getting to work, finding a spouse, having children, worrying about one's future, and all the rest. But now, those day-to-day activities are filled with the slogans, ideas, and worldview of the totalitarian state, where a primary aim of the regime is to make its subjects internalize these slogans, ideas, and worldviews. To put it another way, a typical person will think, "what do I need to do in order to make the best life for my children?" The totalitarian regime wants the "New Man" to instead think, "what do I need to do in order to make my children the best vessels for advancing the State?"

Across totalitarian regimes, one part of daily life that remains notably consistent is the increase in regimentation: schedules, activities, places one can and cannot go, and the like become increasingly disciplined and regulated by the government, as well as by other people in society. In some of these governments, your job is determined by the state. In many totalitarian systems, there are internal passports. A person's ability to go from one place to another is limited, and going elsewhere requires permission from the government (and, in effect, the Party). Work itself is regimented. Along with the usual activities, there will be times set aside for ideological indoctrination, mandatory "voluntary" extra work outside of usual business hours, and required participation in "spontaneous" mass parades (usually either to praise the leadership or denounce some form of Enemy). Depending on the needs and aims of the regime, a typical day might also require some physical training (such as morning calisthenics or the like) and other forms of discipline activities. While many of these activities might technically be "voluntary," lack of participation can result in rather unpleasant sanctions. In the best of times, it could mean more work, less pay, losing one's job, or the like, while in harder times, lack of participation can result in visits from the secret police, arrests, being shipped off to work camps, or worse. Note that these punishments would not be limited to the non-participant alone, but would also put a shadow over the reputation (and safety) of friends and family members.

The majority of the population goes along with this strict new order even if they are not pleased with it. It is just "how things are." These people may heavily dislike the system but are limited in what they can do about it. Most people will have families and/or friends, and would reasonably fear that any resistance would have harsh ramifications for them as well. Such individuals may even assist the regime in some ways, such as providing information on other "less loyal" coworkers as a way to protect their own loved ones. But even if there is an individual who lacks family/friends, or who thinks that resistance is still correct even with the costs, such an individual will likely still follow the demands of the regime. Propaganda, discipline, regimentation, and the omnipresent ideological notion that the current society is "inevitable" typically leads to a high degree of "atomization." Atomization refers to a society where the individual is effectively isolated from connections with others and thus stands alone in relation to the government and society. Lacking any other type of association or institutions upon which one can trust, the individual feels alone and vulnerable. It would be akin to the feeling of a woman on a beach seeing a 50-foot tsunami heading straight toward her. There is no way to even delay the wave, no place to run. So, too, in the totalitarian society. The State seems overwhelming and invincible, all typical associations (clubs, work, pubs, and the like) are under the control of the Party and government, and indeed even one's own family members may be acting as informants for the government and would relay any "disloyal" comments a person might make. Turning again to a literary example, Winston (the protagonist of *1984*) perfectly encapsulates the experience of a person in an atomized, totalitarian society. For the government, this outcome is preferable. Again, human beings are social creatures, so an atomized individual is more likely to turn to the state and the Party to gain the connections most humans desire.

But, with all that being said, we also must note that, for a not small number of people, totalitarian regimes can provide some benefits. As odd as it may sound to us, many regular people saw opportunities in the new totalitarian systems. Certainly, members of the vanguard party benefited. After spending years outside of power (or indeed, even being hunted by the police), these individuals had control over the state. Beyond power, there would be numerous perks to being a party member, including access to better jobs, a better chance of

moving up the ranks in one's occupation, and usually greater ease
in life (access to better stores/goods, getting better housing, and so
forth). But even for those outside the core Party, many totalitarian
regimes provided benefits to various populations, leading to support for the new governments (even if many of these people did
not fully "buy in" to the reigning ideology, at least initially). Most
totalitarian regimes, if they are able, will engage in many large-scale
industrial and infrastructure projects upon taking power as a means
of increasing the country's power as well as advancing the totalitarian ideology.[10] Whether this involves the various "Five Year Plans"
in Stalin's Soviet Union, or the creation of things like the Autobahn
in Germany under the Nazis, the overall economic power of various
totalitarian regimes will increase in some periods, and the general
population may get some benefits from these improvements. However, this major push for quick technological and economic advancement has its costs as well. While infrastructure improvements would
be appealing after years of crisis and instability, these changes are built
on the backs of the population through rationing and severe regimentation. Despite these harder times, social shifts that arise in these
regimes can provide some benefits (and thus, support) from larger
parts of the population. Whether it is purging out the bourgeoisie
and "kulaks" (in places like the Soviet Union) or Jews and "degener-
ates" (such as in Nazi Germany), a large number of occupations, jobs,
and positions opened up for various parts of society. After removing
these "Enemy" populations from jobs (and more), the regime needs
someone to fill these positions. For a goodly number of people, the
totalitarian regime offered a chance at social mobility, or at "moving up" to new/better jobs and greater types of material benefits. In
turning to something like Stalin's Soviet Union, Fitzpatrick describes
how various types of (properly "loyal") workers, peasants, and others
had access to new types of employment – and social status – after the
various purges of "Enemy" populations.[11] One sees a similar dynamic
in Nazi Germany, particularly in intellectual and cultural areas of
work.[12] One could fully expect that similar types of mobility would
show themselves in the Islamic State and other types of totalitarian
governments.

There are some other people who support and benefit from the
state, although often they are not directly part of the totalitarian
regime. They are not government officials (although they may act as

informants), and they are not party members. Instead, they are people who combine intrusiveness, viciousness, and a strong inclination to align with the "Right Side" of society (which, in practice, means aligning with whatever institution or group has power). A shorter manner of describing these people would be "busybodies": individuals inclined toward meddling in other people's lives, but framing this nosiness – to others as well as to themselves – as performing a socially beneficial service. Every society that reaches a certain size will probably have "busybodies," where these individuals are an annoyance and can create tensions/"drama" where none are needed nor desired, but the damage from such people tends to be limited to their immediate circle of acquaintances. Within a totalitarian system, however, "busybodies" become notable instruments for maintaining surveillance and fear within the society. Beyond keeping up the fear of surveillance (knowing that a "busybody" could be listening in and report you if, for instance, you make an off-hand joke about Hitler's mustache or Mao's double-chin), these individuals help the atomization process. People are likely to try to "blend in" and "disappear" among the masses as much as possible to avoid giving a prickly busybody (who takes a disliking to them) from finding some "disloyalty" to report. For our purposes, we merely need to note these people exist. As for why these busybodies find any pleasure in their actions, it is perhaps best to leave that to the psychologists.

Certainly, totalitarian regimes depend upon a great deal of acceptance from their populations. But there is a reason why people usually associate "totalitarianism" with "terror" and the like. How does terror fit in with what we've discussed thus far? It is to this topic we turn next.

Totalitarianism and Terror

Chapter 1 noted how people often associate totalitarianism with terror and fear. One of the most famous ideas from Orwell's *1984* is "BIG BROTHER IS WATCHING YOU" – the notion of an all-watching, all-knowing, and all-controlling government that shapes the minds of its subjects. While the day-to-day lives of many people may not necessarily be under this constant level of oppressive observation, it is often the perception of the population that such surveillance and potential coercion exists. Indeed, a totalitarian regime very much wants its subjects to have this belief. That said, terror is a core part of totalitarian regimes. While the amount of terror varies between totalitarian states, a system of this type simply cannot exist for any real length of time without it.

Terror and brutality are not in themselves unique to totalitarianism. Multiple different types of government will use terror at one point or another. Our intuitive connection of terror and totalitarianism, however, is not incorrect. Moreso than other types of regimes, the reliance on terror is wider and deeper within totalitarian systems than others. While the next section will focus more on the role of killing within totalitarian regimes, here we will talk about terror itself. What do we mean by "terror"? When various scholars try to define terrorism, they usually emphasize that terrorists use violence to further some political or ideological aim. But it is important to note three elements that are also part of terror as part of totalitarian practice (as well as in some acts of terrorists). The first element is the *arbitrary nature* of terror. In other words, it often appears to those who are under a terror regime that there is no rhyme or reason to why some people are arrested or "disappear" while others are not. It can have the sense of randomness one usually associates with a natural event, like lightning strikes or tornadoes. While there are some precautions one can take to lessen the chance of being "hit" (be it by a lightning bolt or by the secret police in the dead of night), there is no way to fully protect one's self nor to fully predict if one is out of harm's way. The second element is the *intentionally ambiguous nature* of what will happen to a person who falls on the wrong side of the regime. If the secret police come for you, will you only face an interrogation about people you know? Will you be tortured? Will you be accused of helping the Enemy populations? Will you be sent to a "reeducation camp" or some other type of concentration camp? Will you be executed, be it after or a trial or just along the road? Will anyone ever know what happened to you, or will you just "disappear" while those who did know you will avoid mentioning your name (to avoid the same treatment)? The third element is a bit harder to sum up in a phrase, but perhaps we could call it the *lack of salvation*. People caught in the net of terror have little hope that they will be found "not guilty" or released, short of some major change in the regime itself (such as utter defeat in war or the death of the leader). To be arrested is to be guilty, even if the arrestee has little idea of what "crime" s/he has committed. Indeed, it could very well be that what was praised last week has become a crime today, and retroactively so. To give an example from the Soviet Union, if one had praised "hero of the Revolution" Trotsky back when he still was in good standing, that praise could make you guilty of being a "capitalist saboteur" once Trotsky fell out of favor. While the past may "change" (with the regime changing around its official history, such as moving Trotsky from being a major player in the Russian Revolution toward being a minor and traitorous one instead), any individual's past does not. In such a situation, people living under terror have no real means of ensuring loyalty in the past will not be reinterpreted as treason later on.

Again, ideology drives the totalitarian party and regime, which means that "purity" becomes an important concern for both. "Purity" here means holding the "correct" views on the ideology (and keeping up with the changes on what "correct" means), but also means maintaining loyalty to the Party and its mission (in the Soviet system, this was called *partiinost'*, or "party-spiritedness"). For most totalitarian regimes, terror is an "undercurrent" in the society, while only at certain points does it become an all-encompassing fear. For instance, while the fear of being found an "enemy of the state" existed throughout the reigns of Stalin and Mao, it was during Stalin's "Great Purge" or "Great Terror" and Mao's "Cultural Revolution" that terror came to the forefront, dominating the minds and activities of effectively all of the residents within these respective regimes. For many totalitarian states, there will be some level of terror near the beginning of the Party taking power – in order to eliminate other contenders for government control – followed by a comparative downgrading of terror for a time. But at some point, the need for terror will arise again. Here is where "purity" comes in. As things become more complicated for the regime – which can include internal disputes among the leadership, unanticipated ideological associations arising among the lower parts of the party, economic or social difficulties, and other such things – dangerous questions regarding the future of the regime may start developing. One major response to these issues is the increased emphasis by the government to kill "Enemies," while another is to purge "hidden" opponents of the regime, which could include disguised members of the "Enemy" population but also includes "fellow-travelers" and other "disloyal" parts of the population. Note that the regime considers these threats as existential. In the Party's mind, the ability of these "Enemies" and their allies to act makes them an extreme danger to the very existence of the totalitarian state, and thus to the creation of the "New Society." As such, there is no desire to be conciliatory. In the totalitarians' minds, they are creating paradise on Earth. After all, if you could bring an end to all oppression and pain, would it not be worth rounding up, killing, or "thought-reforming" millions of people?

A major, and obvious, fear under a regime of terror is death. Again, we will talk more about killing in the next section. But there are other things that make these terrors so daunting, and indeed can often be seen as worse than death itself. Unfortunately, humanity is rather creative in finding ways to inflict pain on other humans, and totalitarian regimes are masters of these most dark arts. Upon arrest and depending upon the regime, the arrestee could be beaten, tortured through electrocution, confined in dirty and too-small cells, raped, repeatedly awakened every 15–20 minutes for days (or even weeks) on end for "interviews," subjected to stress positions, made to eat feces, or other types of indignities. If one was sent to a work camp, the arrestee may spend years – or even decades – in substandard conditions, facing slow and painful death from inhospitable conditions, disease, overwork, or starvation. In many cases, the arrestee may be sent to a "re-education" camp for "thought reform," put to work, harangued constantly with propaganda, and required to repeatedly write self-biographies of one's activities (and being tortured or sanctioned for even slight changes from one self-biography to the next), all with the aim of shaping the arrestee's mind in such a way that it accepts the regime (and its ideology) wholeheartedly.[13] Much of the population will never face these tortures themselves, but are still influenced by them. After noticing various friends or coworkers "disappearing," after hearing about associates denounced as traitors, after interacting with someone who had been in the "care" of the Cheka or Gestapo, and after hearing numerous rumors about what happens to those who are arrested, most people will live in utter fear of being taken away and will put maximum effort into appearing – and perhaps being – good, dutiful "comrades" to the totalitarian regime.

Beyond the perceived "Enemies" of the totalitarian system, terror was frequently applied within the Party itself. Partially, these purges and terrors were a direct result of the totalitarian party's success.

Being a member of the party would mean greater opportunities for better jobs and higher prestige, so numerous people who joined near the time when the party took control or just afterward did so not from loyalty or ideological dedication, but from rather more pedestrian motivations. Party leaders were certainly aware of this problem. Likewise, party leaders were also aware of internal divisions within the party, sometimes based on ideological differences, while other times based on loyalty to various specific leaders (usually, these two aspects overlapped). An early and spectacular purge of this type is the notorious "Night of the Long Knives" in Germany from 30 June to 2 July 1934, where numerous members and leaders of the Nazi SA (*Sturmabteilung*, "Storm Detachment") were murdered by the Nazi regime, including Ernst Röhm.[14] Even more notorious was the "Great Purge" or "Great Terror" in the Soviet Union under Stalin.[15] One of the most striking, and disconcerting, parts of the Terror involved the "show trials" of various Party members, including members who had been part of the Politburo or other major committees. Two elements in the show trials are notable. First, these trials required a belief in extensive conspiracies of "counter-revolutionaries" that included some of the most important and respected Communists in the regime. One had to believe that individuals who had been major Bolsheviks in the Russian Revolution had betrayed the Soviet Union (and the whole Marxist-Leninist ideology) by working for the capitalists, the Fascists, or others. The second notable element is how many of these figures – Nikolai Bukharin, a former Politburo member, being the main example – confessed to what sounded like insane charges. These confessions created significant levels of cognitive dissonance. On the one hand, the charges seemed ludicrous (such as that there were extensive "Trotskyite" conspiracies responsible for everything from attempted assassinations to decreased economic productivity); but on the other hand, these individuals confessed to them. Were the charges true, then? Did Bukharin (for instance) have such great *partiinost'* that he would willingly make such mad confessions "for the good of the Party"? Did the Stalinists have forms of coercion and torture so horrible that they could convince someone to confess to capital crimes? Terror is made all the more frightening when it can strike even high Party members.

But if terror can strike almost anyone, what about killing? Certainly, horrific numbers of people are murdered during terror periods within totalitarian states. But killing in totalitarianism also often entails full extermination of populations, to which we now turn.

The Vice of Killing

In addition to extensive surveillance, propaganda, and terror, most people associate totalitarian regimes with massive levels of state-directed murder. The genocidal actions of the Nazi regime against the Jews, the sheer number of people killed in Communist China under Mao's rule (with estimates of deaths between 30 to 60 million people, if not more),[16] and the slaughter of approximately one-fifth (if not more) of Cambodia's population within a four-year period under the Khmer Rouge are among the most infamous and notorious examples of totalitarianism's murderous actions.[17] But, as we noted in Chapter 1, state-sponsored killing is not a uniquely totalitarian activity. Dictatorships and other types of regimes also engage in quite of bit of murder. Additionally, there are some totalitarian regimes that do not engage in similar forms of mass murder, with Fascist Italy being the primary example (although it is possibly an outlier). And yet, the connection made between totalitarianism and killing is not accidental or coincidental. What traits and/or motivations might distinguish totalitarian policies on killing from other regimes?

We can point to two traits that provide such a distinction. The first trait is the motivation for killing, which brings us back to the ideological elements discussed in Chapter 2. For most totalitarian ideational systems, the "Enemy" population is inherently and irredeemably against the "progress" of History. These populations cannot be convinced or converted, and will always remain a counter-revolutionary threat to the "New Society." In effect, the very *existence* of these populations presents an ongoing danger to the "New Man." One can see an implicit logic toward complete extermination of the Enemy population. This ideological element supplies a noteworthy distinction from dictatorial forms of killing. Dictatorships will also seek to wipe out oppositional groups and populations, but the aim is to generally demoralize and terrorize such populations into submission. Once the potential danger of these populations is degraded, dictatorships will generally pull back from killing. For these regimes, the aim is the maintenance of power, rather than the construction of some "New Society," and they would generally prefer to have a demoralized population that is still engaged in work (be it building infrastructure, constructing weapons for the military, working on farms, or what have you) rather than expending a great deal of time, money, and effort in totally eliminating them.

A second trait develops as a result of the problems faced by a totalitarian regime and how these problems are perceived through totalitarian ideology. The ruling party of a totalitarian system truly believes that it understands the "science" of History, knows the "direction" of History, and can provide the proper guidance for the creation of the "New Society" and the "New Man." But what happens when things do not go according to plan? Why would (for instance) the "world revolution" not occur, or a classless system not result in higher efficiency and productivity, or that "master race" has not "awoken" to its potential? The totalitarian party can accept that it made some smaller "tactical" errors or did not completely assess available information, but the Party cannot accept that it is wrong on fundamental points. In this view, problems cannot be the result of the theory being wrong, nor can it be caused by the incompetence or corruption of the true "vanguard" or world-historic population, nor can these problems be the result of the complexities of life and reality. Instead, totalitarian regimes believe that problems must be intentionally caused by people intending to undermine the "New Society." Their ideologies already have an "Enemy" population in mind, so these groups become the "authors" of problems in the system. These populations are inherently "counter-revolutionary," so they "of course" will do everything in their power to destroy the world-historic population and its vanguard. Obviously, one can see how this type of reasoning can be a form of blame-shifting. But we should avoid being overly cynical in our estimation of whether totalitarian leaders and Party members were merely being Machiavellian. Instead, it seems that most of these individuals were "double-minded," as it were. Yes, they would often cynically point to these "Enemy" populations as the "true" cause of problems, but also simultaneously believed that these populations were, in some sense, actually responsible for the problems the regime faced. Once again, the inherent logic of totalitarian ideologies lends itself to exterminating enemy groups, and the inevitable rise of problems provides additional "evidence" to totalitarian rulers that the enemy population is dangerous in its very existence. The most notorious example is the role of Jews as the ongoing "Enemy" for the Nazis, but one can also look at the "kulaks" in Stalin's Soviet Union as another example of a population blamed for the regime's own failings.

This second trait is usually associated with the term "scapegoating." Scapegoating is certainly not an unfamiliar activity in life, and particularly in political life. In our own lives, scapegoating is often either a means of avoiding blame or a type of rationalization we tell ourselves to avoid responsibility. In politics, scapegoating often acts in similar ways. Shifting blame onto some other group, particularly a group that is already facing legal, social, and other types of sanctions, both eases the burden of responsibility on those in leadership positions and gives some reassurance to the general population ("These problems aren't the result of some major systemic problem or of us being wrong. If we just get rid of those *bad people* who are screwing things up, things will work as expected."). One can see the obvious connection of scapegoating to totalitarianism's penchant for killing. But one should be cautious about putting too much emphasis on the scapegoating element. There can be a tendency to view the totalitarian motivation for mass murder as simply a type of psychological quirk, or rather as a horrific level of immaturity. While this notion does have the benefit of making us feel better about ourselves, it is less helpful for understanding. Arguing that it is "mere" scapegoating taken to an extreme is more an example of "dollar-store psychoanalysis" than useful insight.

Given the sheer amount of propaganda, surveillance, terror, and killing, it seems that a totalitarian state would either collapse almost immediately under its own coercive weight or could go on indefinitely. And yet, totalitarian regimes can last for many decades, dying not immediately but also not living permanently. But is such a regime always totalitarian? It is to this question we now turn.

Life After Totalitarianism

One of the great fears expressed in many dystopian novels on totalitarianism is that, upon gaining enough power and control, a totalitarian regime could exist permanently, with little to no means by which a ruled population could free itself (or indeed, would even *want* to free itself). A famous phrase from *1984* reflects this fear: "If you want a picture of the future, imagine a boot stamping on a human face – forever."[18] And yet, with a few notable exceptions, most totalitarian regimes that have existed, exist no more. How do totalitarian states end?

Most of us are familiar with totalitarian regimes ending through external actions, specifically from defeat in war. Fascist Italy and Nazi Germany ceased to be totalitarian systems when they were overtaken by Allied forces in the Second World War, and their societies reconstructed by the victors. The level of reconstruction varied between Italy and Germany, for various reasons. The Fascists had never managed fully to eliminate some other power centers in Italy, and thus many parts of Italian society were not as enmeshed with the Fascist system and ideology. The Nazis, on the other hand, had greater efficiency in removing competitors and solidifying power. Moreover, the end of the war resulted in the new competitive alignment of the "West" (headed by the United States) and the "East" (under the command of the Soviet Union), with Germany's territory acting as the border between the two blocs. As such, both sides put a great deal of money and effort into reshaping their respective territories into a Western-style representative democracy (for West Germany) or Communist-style totalitarian system (for East Germany). Had Fascist Italy or Nazi Germany lived to see the end of the Second World War, it is unclear how long they would have continued existing. While these governments had extensive propaganda, terror, and surveillance systems in place, could they persist after the death (natural or otherwise) of the *Duce* or the *Führer*? Totalitarianism's death by external action might give us some clarity in terms of the regime type's weaknesses in war, but it does not help us in understanding how a totalitarian regime might change internally over time.

The Soviet Union provides a different example of totalitarianism's end. While the Soviet system itself ceased to exist in 1991, was it totalitarian throughout its existence? When people think of Soviet totalitarianism, they primarily think of Stalin's reign from 1924 to 1953, and some might also remember parts of Lenin's rule as well. Additionally, some might associate Soviet totalitarianism with the response to the "Prague Spring" in 1968 or other similar time periods. But what of other times? Some scholars, especially the interesting studies by Juan J. Linz,[19] have classified these systems as "post-totalitarian." In many ways, the post-totalitarian system is rather similar to a dictatorship or a ruling oligarchy. While the totalitarian ideology is still the official ideology of the regime, very few people (including the leadership) actually believe in it anymore. The post-totalitarian state, like many dictatorships, is more concerned with holding onto power and maintaining the status quo, and thus tends to show a greater interest in power politics (or, in more typical language, Machiavellianism) than in ideological disputes or creating the "New Society."

But while there are significant overlaps between post-totalitarian systems and other authoritarian systems, there remain some large differences. First, the institutional structures of totalitarianism still exist, even if they are less effective or generally unused. Reactivating already existing systems is much simpler – in terms of time, effort, and labor – than attempting to create them, and this holds true for the organizational, mass media, surveillance, and terror structures within totalitarian and post-totalitarian states. The operating systems, state agencies, and training needed for totalitarian activities remain within the post-totalitarian society and can be used to a greater or lesser extent, as needed. Moreover, the people living within a post-totalitarian state – whether rulers or ruled – are very aware of this ability to renew totalitarian institutions. Some of the most notorious or well-known agencies involved in totalitarian terror might be downgraded or renamed, but the infrastructure of them, and the personnel in them, remain and can be brought into action again. Even if these previous totalitarian agencies are not put into full force, their continued existence can shape how a post-totalitarian government operates. This can lead to some comparatively unusual government systems. For instance, China's political system shifted into what could be called a form of "decentralized authoritarianism"[20] after Mao's death, which is a rather atypical form of government and one that is hard to envision coming into existence within a typical authoritarian state. Second, the totalitarian ideology is still technically the source of legitimacy and guidance for the regime, and can potentially rise to prominence again. Ideology in post-totalitarian regimes often seem more like a loyalty marker than as a belief system. Even if people do not believe in the ideology, mouthing fealty to it shows proper dedication to the State. But the continued existence and familiarity of the ideology can spawn new "revivals" of it within the post-totalitarian state, bringing it back into a more blatantly totalitarian form. To use a religious comparison again, it would be rather like a denomination where the creeds and rituals had become rather rote, with people just "going through the motions" as it were, only to be reenergized through a revivalist movement of some type or another. For instance, this would likely be the prospective of many Christians to the Protestant Reformation begun by Martin Luther in 1517. This type of thing can also occur in a post-totalitarian system. Once again, China presents a useful (if somewhat unique) example. One could view the time after the "Great Leap Forward" (which caused tens of millions of deaths from starvation) as a more "post-totalitarian" period within the history of the People's Republic. But in 1966, totalitarian elements sprang to life once again with the highly ideological "Cultural Revolution." This movement could be viewed as a cynical ploy by Mao to increase his power within the government – and there is some truth to this view – but the ideological emphasis also means that this movement went well beyond just power plays in the Politburo. The ideology allowed for the "Great Awakening" of the Maoist totalitarian system.

In practice, Communist states seem more likely to become "post-totalitarian" than other types of totalitarian systems. One big reason for this difference is historical. As noted previously, most of the prominent non-Communist totalitarian states find themselves on the losing end of a major war, and a different system is put in place not by the ruling party, but by the victors in the conflict. But there is also a structural reason for this difference as well. As discussed earlier, Communist states are usually ruled (at least in theory) by a "Politburo" with various members, even if one member (Stalin, Mao, or the like) effectively is dominant, while other types of totalitarian systems (especially nation- and race-based ones) focus on the "leadership principle" under one ruler who epitomizes the "Nation" or "Race" in some way (where this leader exemplifies the "feel" and "vitality" of the nation or race). What happens when the leader ceases to rule, be it from death or disability? In Communist totalitarian systems, the Politburo provides the means of succession (in other words, transfer of office from one person to another). The committee structure gives a greater level of stability by laying out a system for choosing new rulers. "Leadership principle" totalitarian regimes, on the other hand, generally lack such a clear-cut method for succession. Since the leader is in many ways almost like a demi-god in the government, these regimes usually do not have a firm system for finding a new leader (assuming that another such pseudo-divinity would "grace" the country), other than an ambiguous hope that the "New Society" will put forward a "New Man" who can take on this role. Just as strange women lying in ponds distributing swords is not a sensible manner of selecting new leaders in government, a vague hope that a new Führer will "pop up" when needed is no way to keep a government going. Even if a "leadership principle" totalitarian regime did not meet its end in war, it is questionable whether it could even exist as a post-totalitarian system after the death of its leader.

Conclusion

Now you have trudged through four chapters of abstract discussion on totalitarianism as an ideology, a party/movement, and as a government. Well done. But just as abstract discussions of mammalian or avian biological classes do not give one much insight to the specific nature and activities of raccoons or vultures, abstract musing on government systems need more "fleshing out" to truly understand them. It is now time to turn away from broad theoretical discussions of totalitarianism and toward historical, specific cases of totalitarianism as they have existed, and to see how all of these theoretical discussions "fit" into the actual practice of totalitarianism.

Summing Up

• Totalitarian states can be viewed as their own "regime type," just as democracy and monarchy describe a "family" of governments with fundamental similarities.
• A totalitarian government is ruled through the vanguard Party, and it seeks to overtake (or eliminate) any sources of authority or influence outside of the regime itself and its ideology.
• Life in a totalitarian society is saturated with propaganda, blanketed with surveillance, punctuated with periods of terror, and often significantly atomized.
• As totalitarian ideology perceives its "Enemy" populations as irredeemable and implacable foes, there is an inherent tendency

in totalitarian regimes toward mass murder and genocide as a means to exterminate these "threats."
• Totalitarian governments can change into "post-totalitarian" states, which take on many traits of authoritarian systems but also maintain the structures of totalitarianism.

Suggested Reading

The "Suggested Reading" sections of the previous chapters have noted how texts on specific ideologies or organizations outnumber those on totalitarian ideas/movements in general. That remains very much the same when looking at totalitarian governments. One finds a much greater variety of analyses (both generally as well as on particular elements of any given system) when looking at specific totalitarian regimes. In terms of the Soviet Union as well as other states of the Eastern Bloc, consider Hoffman (2011) and Suny (2011), among others. For Fascist Italy, Bosworth (1998) is a helpful beginning text. A good overview of the Nazi regime can be found in Burleigh (2000). A useful comparison of the Fascist and Nazi regimes is found in De Grand (2004). In considering the rule of Mao in China, a short source is Cheek (2002). In considering the Khmer Rouge rule in Cambodia, see Chandler (1999). For the Iranian regime, see Axworthy (2013), and see Cockburn (2015) on the Islamic State. Some books also provide comparisons between different types of totalitarian governments. Looking especially at their party-rule systems, an excellent source is Unger (1974), but also consider Gray (2020).

Notes

1. My thanks to Paul Gray for this observation.
2. Azrael (1966) gives a good sense of how the "nuts-and-bolts" of administration works in such a system.
3. In the Nazi case, this was sometimes called the "dual state" form of government. Although it has some questionable interpretations at points, a notable examination of this system is Fraenkel (2010).
4. The Italian Fascist and German Nazi regimes are good examples of these limits. While they took power in 1922 and 1933, respectively, it took years for both governments to gain full control. Indeed, the Fascists never managed to gain complete control before the Allied invasion in 1943. The Republic of

Saló (1943–1945) gave the Italian Fascists somewhat more leeway, but, even here, they were under the protection (and demands) of Nazi Germany.

5. For instance, see Clark (2011), Ben-Ghiat (2001) Berezin (1997), and Ma (1995).
6. Shlapentokh (1988).
7. Siemens (2013).
8. Yang (2016).
9. Stites (1989).
10. A. James Gregor notes this tendency, calling it a form of "developmental dictatorship." See Gregor (1979).
11. Fitzpatrick (1999).
12. Some useful works include Ingrao (2013) and Dennis (2012), among many others.
13. For a useful discussion on these methods in Maoist China, see Lifton (1961).
14. Among others, see Hancock (2008): 154–166.
15. Conquest (2008).
16. Dikötter (2010); see also MacFarquhar and Schoenhals (2006).
17. See Courtois et al. (1999).
18. Orwell (1981): 239.
19. Linz (2000).
20. Landry (2008).

Bibliography

Axworthy, Michael. 2013. *Revolutionary Iran: A History of the Islamic Republic.* Oxford: Oxford University Press.

Azrael, Jeremy R. 1966. *Managerial Power and Soviet Politics.* Cambridge: Harvard University Press.

Ben-Ghiat, Ruth. 2001. *Fascist Modernities: Italy, 1922–1945.* Berkeley: University of California Press.

Berezin, Mabel. 1997. *Making of the Fascist Self: The Political Culture of Interwar Italy.* Ithaca: Cornell University Press.

Bosworth, R. J. B. 1998. *The Italian Dictatorship: Problems and Perspectives in the Interpretation of Mussolini and Fascism.* London: Arnold.

Burleigh, Michael. 2000. *The Third Reich: A New History.* New York: Hill and Wang.

Chandler, David P. 1999. *Brother Number One: A Political Biography of Pol Pot.* Boulder: Westview Press.

Cheek, Timothy. 2002. *Mao Zedong and China's Revolutions: A Brief History with Documents.* Boston: Bedford/St. Martin's.

Clark, Katerina. 2011. *Moscow, the Fourth Rome: Stalinism, Cosmopolitanism, and the Evolution of Soviet Culture, 1931–1941.* Cambridge: Harvard University Press.

Cockburn, Patrick. 2015. *The Rise of the Islamic State: ISIS and the New Sunni Revolution*. London: Verso.

Conquest, Robert. 2008. *The Great Terror: A Reassessment*. Fortieth Anniversary Edition. Oxford: Oxford University Press.

Courtois, Stephane, Nicholas Werth, Jean-Louis Panne, Andrzej Packowski, Karel Bartosek, and Jean-Louis Margolin. 1999. *The Black Book of Communism: Crimes, Terror, Repression*. Mark Kramer, trans. Cambridge: Harvard University Press.

De Grand, Alexander. 2004. *Fascist Italy and Nazi Germany: The 'Fascist' Style of Rule*. New York: Routledge.

Dennis, David B. 2012. *Inhumanities: Nazi Interpretations of Western Culture*. Cambridge: Cambridge University Press.

Dikötter, Frank. 2010. *Mao's Great Famine: The History of China's Most Devastating Catastrophe, 1958–1962*. New York: Walker & Company.

Fitzpatrick, Sheila. 1999. *Everyday Stalinism: Ordinary Life in Extraordinary Times: Soviet Russia in the 1930s*. Oxford: Oxford University Press.

Fraenkel, Ernst. 2010. *The Dual State: A Contribution to the Theory of Dictatorship*. E. A. Shils, trans. Clark: The Lawbook Exchange, Ltd.

Gray, Phillip W. 2020. *Vanguardism: Ideology and Organization in Totalitarian Politics*. New York: Routledge.

Gregor, A. James. 1979. *Italian Fascism and Developmental Dictatorship*. Princeton: Princeton University Press.

Hancock, Eleanor. 2008. *Ernst Röhm: Hitler's SA Chief of Staff*. New York: Palgrave Macmillan.

Hoffman, David L. 2011. *Cultivating the Masses: Modern State Practices and Soviet Socialism 1914–1939*. Ithaca: Cornell University Press.

Ingrao, Christian. 2013. *Believe & Destroy: Intellectuals in the SS War Machine*. Andrew Brown, trans. Cambridge: Polity Press.

Landry, Pierre F. 2008. *Decentralized Authoritarianism in China: The Communist Party's Control of Local Elites in the Post-Mao Era*. Cambridge: Cambridge University Press.

Lifton, Robert Jay. 1961. *Thought Reform and the Psychology of Totalism: A Study of "Brainwashing" in China*. New York: W. W. Norton & Company.

Linz, Juan J. 2000. *Totalitarian and Authoritarian Regimes*. Boulder: Lynne Rienner Publishers.

Ma, Bo. 1995. *Blood and Sunset: A Memoir of the Chinese Cultural Revolution*. New York: Penguin Books.

MacFarquhar, Roderick, and Michael Schoenhals. 2006. *Mao's Last Revolution*. Cambridge: Belknap Press.

Orwell, George. 1981. *1984*. New York: Plume.

Shlapentokh, Vladimir. 1988. "The Stakhanovite Movement: Changing Perceptions over Fifty Years." *Journal of Contemporary History* 23(2): 259–276.

Siemens, Daniel. 2013. *The Making of a Nazi Hero: The Murder and Myth of Horst Wessel*. London: I. B. Tauris.

Stites, Richard. 1989. *Revolutionary Dreams: Utopian Visions and Experimental Life in the Russian Revolution*. New York: Oxford University Press.

Suny, Ronald Grigor. 2011. *The Soviet Experiment: Russia, the USSR, and the Successor States*. New York: Oxford University Press.

Unger, Aryeh L. 1974. *The Totalitarian Party: Party and People in Nazi Germany and Soviet Russia*. Cambridge: Cambridge University Press.

Yang, Jisheng. 2016. *The World Turned Upside Down: A History of the Chinese Cultural Revolution*. New York: Farrar, Straus and Giroux.

5

TOTALITARIANISM IN HISTORY

So far, we have discussed totalitarianism rather broadly and abstractly. Aside from some concrete examples used here and there in the previous chapters, "totalitarianism" might appear more like an apparition or a ghost, frightening yet spectral. Certainly, the world would be a much nicer place if totalitarianism was merely a fictional construct – a fantasy monster like Dracula or the Mothman. Alas, totalitarianism has been, and may be again, a quite real thing. In this chapter, we will go over totalitarianism within history, making particular note of major totalitarian regimes, movements, parties, thinkers, and the like, noting some of the "prehistory" that set the stage for totalitarianism's growth as well as some of the major examples of it.

A natural question would be: "what was the first totalitarian regime?" If one wished to be viciously literal, Fascist Italy should likely claim that title, as it was the first regime to explicitly declare itself to be totalitarian in aim and structure. That said, various systems (political, social, economic, and so forth) often exist for quite some time before they receive a specific name and are recognized as a distinct type. So, too, with totalitarianism. But this does complicate matters, because it becomes less clear what we could call the first totalitarian regime, much less the first totalitarian ideology or movement. For instance, Norman Cohn notes the similarities between some totalitarian movements of the last two centuries with various millennialist movements in the medieval period.[1] Should these be our starting point? This would seem to start things too early. Totalitarianism depends upon a certain level of mass political involvement to exist, which places it within the modern period.[2] As we delve into the history of totalitarianism, we will address the issue and others.

DOI: 10.4324/9781003254232-5

This chapter is separated into three sections. The first section discusses some of the developments in the seventeenth to early twentieth centuries that helped create conditions for totalitarianism, including ideological/philosophical changes as well as the "proto-totalitarian" regime. The second part examines the "Golden Age" of totalitarianism, going from about the end of the First World War until the early 1950s. The third section notes changes in totalitarianism after the "Golden Age" until the present, noting how ideologies and organizational forms shifted during the remainder of the twentieth century and going into the twenty-first century. We have much to cover, so let us begin with a "prehistory" of totalitarianism.

"Prehistory" of Totalitarianism

Pinpointing the "first" totalitarian regime is less simple than one might suppose, and finding the "first" totalitarian parties and ideologies is even harder. One could point to some periods of time in the "Consistory" of Geneva (from 1541 to around 1546) as being proto-totalitarian in nature.[3] Likewise, others might consider some of the actions during the First and Second English Civil Wars (1642–1646 and 1648–1549, respectively), as well as during the "Rump Parliament" (1649–1653) and the Protectorate under Oliver Cromwell (1653–1658) as perhaps being an instance of a totalitarian-like movement or regime, particularly with the formation of the Puritan-infused "New Model Army" in 1645 and its importance until the Stuart Restoration of 1661.[4] However, both of these instances seem a poor fit for the label totalitarian due to the lower nature of technology and the lack of a mass society in these places, as well as some of the specifics of the theologies in these movements/regimes deviating from the norm of later totalitarian systems.

Many of the ideational and technical changes that created for totalitarianism to grow arose later, during the eighteenth century. For intellectual historians, this period represents a high point in the Enlightenment, with the initial publication of the *Encyclopédie* in France in 1751 (and continuing for another 20 years) as a good illustration. Contributors to this large group of volumes included such notable figures as Diderot, Montesquieu, and Voltaire, but one particular author requires particular attention: Jean-Jacques Rousseau (1712–1778). Rousseau was a rather odd man, and his philosophy – or the various ways it has been developed, at least – is similarly peculiar. For many egalitarian thinkers and movements, Rousseau's idea is a shining example of enlightened thinking toward a more democratic and just society.[5] For others, Rousseau's philosophy is a key part of the foundation for totalitarian thinking.[6] While he is perhaps best known for his declaration of the fundamental equality of human beings, there are other elements of his thought that are important in the development of totalitarianism. The first concerns human nature and institutions, especially as he discusses them in Rousseau's *Discourse on Inequality* (published in 1754).[7] This work emphasizes the inherent equality of humanity, but also focuses on human nature – or rather, lack of human nature. For Rousseau, human beings are primarily shaped by the social institutions under which they live. If there is inequality and injustice, it is not because of "original sin" or some other internal elements in humans, but rather because of corrupt institutions (in his view, such as private property). Change the institutions (into a "New Society"), and you change humanity (a "New Man," as it were). The second element, which Rousseau fleshes out in his *Social Contract* (published in 1762),[8] is the idea of the "General Will." While hard to summarize, this "General Will" is reason and justice separated from particularistic interests, standing in contrast to the particular will (with all of its specific eccentricities and interests) of any given person in a society. It is the "General Will" – this abstract yet sovereign "thing" in Rousseau's philosophy – that determines law and right, and those who are out of line with this Will must be forced in line. For later totalitarian ideologies, the general "shape" of this "General Will" would reappear with "world-historic" populations (for instance, that the "Proletariat" has certain interests, even if no specific member of the working class actually has such interests).

Technological and geopolitical changes also occur around this time. For many historians, the mid-1700s is the starting point for the Industrial Revolution, beginning in Britain and then spreading to other parts of Europe and North America. Technological and ideational changes of a radical nature were occurring during this period as well. We've already talked about some of the philosophical transformations in this period, so let's briefly turn to technology and science. Forms of mechanization, the greater use of different energy sources (such as steam, coal, or others), the ability to mass-assemble products, and the advances in transportation technology radically changed day-to-day life for numerous European countries. Perhaps one of the most important results of these technological advances was the increased size and importance of urban populations, and likewise the increased self-identification of the industrial working class as a group (often also known as the "proletariat"). Urban populations already had a notable influence on revolutionary politics, with the French Revolution being a central example,[9] but now the concentration of labor as well as wealth (through newer forms of finance-based capitalism) both enhanced the political importance of cities while simultaneously creating social and economic tensions between the various parts of the urban population. Changes in technology also allowed for what could rightly be called the first truly world war: the Seven Years' War (usually better known in the United States as the French-Indian War), with initial battles beginning around 1754 and concluding in 1763. More advanced technology, greater economic productivity, and the increased centralization of military power in newly emerging nation-states permitted for wider and more extensive conflicts. The various wars – in combination with technological and economic changes – started creating strains within various empires, including setting the stage for the American War of Independence in the 1770s.

These wars also created economic stresses that agitated internal resentments within countries. The best example of this dynamic is in France, where severe levels of military spending, substantial inequalities between rich and poor, and economic downturns resulted in society-rending discontent. Already a "hotspot" of Enlightenment and radical thought despite the absolutist nature of the monarchy, the budget of the French government faced such difficulties in the late 1700s that, on 5 May 1789, King Louis XVI called into session the "Estates-General" in order to gain more funds, starting a series of events that would lead to the setting up of a "National Assembly," the storming of the Bastille, the proclaiming of the "Declarations of the Rights of Man and of the Citizen," and the formation of the Legislative Assembly as the governing power of the country. Welcome to the French Revolution (1789–1799).[10]

The French Revolution becomes more radical in 1792 with the 20 September declaration of the National Convention as the ruler of France, and shocks the world on 21 January 1793, when Louis XVI and others in the monarch's circle are convicted of "High Treason" and beheaded. Through various twists and turns in this tumultuous period, we come to the first major example of a totalitarian regime, or a prototype example of one, when the Jacobin party under Maximilien Robespierre takes full control of the French Revolutionary government in Paris, especially during 1793–1794 (although the most relevant years vary between scholars). Beginning a "Reign of Terror" under the auspices of the "Committee for Public Safety," the Jacobins sought to make a republic of "virtue," which entailed setting up revolutionary tribunals (with few to no protections for the accused) to discover – and execute – various "counterrevolutionaries" and other threats to "the People." Before Robespierre's own execution in mid-1794, thousands met their deaths on guillotines, in prisons, or elsewhere. The French government under the Jacobins would be a "proto-totalitarian" regime. It contained various traits of a typical totalitarian system (influencing mass populations through communication technology, heavy surveillance, a notion of a "New Man," and the like), but these elements were rather underdeveloped. One key difference regards ideology. With the ambiguities in the Revolution itself, the "Reign of Terror" lacked a clear sense of "History" and a clear sense of for whom they fought. Instead, a undifferentiated sense of working for "the People" was all it had. The conclusion of the ongoing French Revolution was the ascension of Napoleon Bonaparte as leader of France, and his extended wars against the rest of Europe that (depending upon one's point of view) either intended to spread the new universal notions of humanity, freedom, and brotherhood to the rest of monarchical Europe, or sought to conquer the rest of the world to ensure French hegemony and spread its new ideology.[11] After Napoleon's final defeat in 1815 after the Battle of Waterloo on 18 June, and the established restoration of the Bourbon monarchy in France in the same year, political revolution rather calmed down in Europe (with one major exception that we will talk about later). Philosophical, technological, and ideological revolution, however, continued at a fast pace.[12]

The French Revolution serves as a major example not only for totalitarianism, but also as a major turning point for European political and social thought in general. Perhaps the greatest ferment in thought was not in France, however, but rather in the Germanic territories. At this point, there was no singular German state, but numerous polities of various sorts. But this political division did not offset the other connections between German-speaking peoples. "Germany was in fact a society of states which shared a common culture and a common intellectual life."[13] This is the period with major works published by Immanuel Kant, Johann Gottlieb Fichte, and others from the German-speaking parts of Europe. It is in the period between 1815 and 1848, when Europe is comparatively "quiet" domestically and internationally (illustrated by the formation of the "Holy Alliance" between Tsarist Russia, the Austrian Empire, and Prussia that sought to prevent revolution internationally), that the ideological shockwave that is the philosophy of Hegel arises. Few thinkers are more important for the ideational shape of totalitarianism.

Hegel's philosophy is, well, "difficult" would be a charitable term for it.[14] During and after the period in which he wrote – from roughly 1807 with the publication of *Philosophy of Mind* until his death in in 1831 – the complexity and opaqueness of his theories and methods resulted in numerous interpretations of Hegel's views. We discussed his notion of "History" and "world-historic" populations in Chapter 2, so here we will focus more on his "dialectical method." While difficult to summarize, Hegel's method postulated that reality, in its progress through History, contains contradictions within it. Against earlier views, such as those from Aristotle that a contradiction in something would indicate error or falseness, Hegel believed that contradictions are inherent in reality as History works itself through to its final actualization. It is when the status quo is confronted by these contradictions that a new, higher form arises. It is not that the status quo remains or that the contradiction takes over, but rather this process (called *Aufhebung*, which itself is variously translated) creates a new whole that integrates these elements and comes into existence. Regardless of what Hegel intended with this "dialectical method," it provided a means for various later thinkers and activists to argue that their own ideologies or political preferences were a part of this "working out" of History's contradictions. Indeed, it is a rather back-handed testament to the influence of Hegel's style of thinking that his intellectual descendants include purely reactionary monarchists and the most radical of revolutionaries. One of the most important tendencies would be called the "Young Hegelians" (or "Left Hegelians"), among them a man named Ludwig Feuerbach, who wrote a major book in 1841 that used Hegelian reasoning as a means of undercutting Christianity.[15] While notable in itself, his book would be particularly influential on another man usually grouped with the "Young Hegelians," Karl Marx (1818–1883).[16]

Beyond Hegel, Marx was also strongly influenced by the radical activities happening during his life, especially those surrounding the revolutions in Europe starting in 1848.[17] These revolts, and the movements involved with them, would influence Marx's thinking. Among the innovations of Marx's thought, he brought Hegel's "march of History" and its "world-historic" populations out of the realm of ideas and away from a purely abstract "actualization" of "Spirit" to the physical, concrete world of economic class and technological change. His main attack on Hegel was that the latter was an "idealist," focused on thought rather than actual reality. It's not that Hegel's method or notion of History was wrong, per se, but instead that it should have focused on concrete dynamics (in Marx's view, the combination of technological change and ownership rules that make up economics), and that the "world-historic" populations were best understood as economic classes. That said, Marx and his regular co-writer, Friedrich Engels, tended to focus more on the theorizing side of things than practical work. Certainly, the theoretical work was far from minor. In 1848, the two wrote what would be known as the *Communist Manifesto*, which summarized many of Marx's ideas into a clearer form and provided the language, rhetoric, and argumentative style for many types of radical thought in the coming decades.[18] Moreover, Marx would be a key member of what would be called the "First International" (founded 1864), which provided one of the first key examples of a working-class-focused party, although it would collapse through the infighting between Marx (who wanted his own ideas to dominate) and Mikhail Bakunin (who aimed to make his form of anarchism the central ideology). For better or worse, Marx's language and style of reasoning would become the backbone of major forms of radicalism in the coming years and would significantly influence later totalitarian movements.

As we reach the latter part of the nineteenth century, a different kind of instability appears in Europe (and beyond). Mass political parties and movements began to form, with one of the most important being the "Second International," spearheaded by the German Social Democratic Party. Additionally, this period was also typified by a new type of terrorism, usually viewed as "anarchist" violence. While notable in the 1880s for political assassinations, it was the 1890s that "became the year of the anarchist terrorist bloodbath, as anarchists hurled explosive devices into crowded cafés, religious processions, and operatic performances where they killed men, women and children."[19] The sheer number and audacity of the attacks (sometimes called "propaganda of the deed") brought particular attention. They included the assassination of Tsar Alexander II (1881), the attack on the Liceu opera house in Barcelona (1893), the assassination of French President Sadi Carnot (1894), the assassination of US President William McKinley (1901), and the bombing on the wedding day of Spanish King Alfonso XIII (1906).[20] This type of violence wasn't limited to anarchists, of course. The Socialist-Revolutionary Party of Russia, formed in 1902, had a "Combat Organization" branch dedicated to terrorist acts, the most famous of which was the assassination of Russian Minister of the Interior Vyacheslav von Plehve in 1904. Both political action and violent action became much greater factors during this time.

It is also at this point that "revisions" begin to form within Marxism.[21] First, with Marx's death in in 1883 (and that of Engels in 1895), it was somewhat of an open question who "spoke" for Marxism, especially as Marx's own voluminous writings could be internally inconsistent, or at least underdeveloped. Second, and rather more daunting, was the problem of addressing failures in his theory. What happens if the proletariat doesn't "rise up" against the bourgeoisie? What if the revolution never comes? It is these types of questions that lead to what A. James Gregor has called the first "Crisis of Marxism."[22] It is in this period of the late nineteenth and early twentieth centuries that one sees many "revisionist" forms of Marxism arise, which sometimes attempted to "modify" Marxism for contemporary circumstances. A variety of these revisions would be the seeds for later totalitarian movements and regimes.

As Engels tended to be viewed as the main theorist for Marxism after Marx's death, Karl Kautsky (1854–1938) took on the role of expressing "orthodox" Marxism, with pride of place going to the German Social Democratic Party, which Kautsky headed. At this point, the "Second International" included a wide variety of political views, ranging from extremists itching to overthrow governments to moderates who would rather resemble Social Democrats of today. One of the first "cracks" in Marxian unity would be the critiques from Party member Eduard Bernstein (1850–1932), who argued that Marx's predictions about the unavoidable and scientific certainty of capitalism's ultimate collapse were unsound. Kautsky (among others, including Lenin) would denounce him for his heterodoxy, although Bernstein's ideas would become influential in forming our more contemporary ideas of social democracy. It's important to note that although Bernstein was critiquing Marx, he did not reject Marxism as a whole. One could say the same of another revisionist, Vladimir Illyich Ulyanov, better known to history as V. I. Lenin (1870–1924). A key difference between them, however, is that Lenin thought he was providing a purified version of Marxism, rather than critiquing it (Lenin always thought he was being orthodox[23]). While Lenin will become a rather important political figure for us later, it is in 1902 that he wrote what would be one of his most influential pamphlets, *What Is To be Done?*[24] In it, Lenin first explicated his view of the "vanguard party" with its "professional revolutionaries," while also emphasizing the importance of the party in "pushing" the proletariat toward its "world-historic" task of making the classless society. A year after this publication, Lenin would go on to split the Russian Social Democratic Party in two, with his faction taking on the name "Bolsheviks."

Lenin and Bernstein, while critiquing or changing Marxism, still viewed themselves as Marxists. Other important thinkers would move away from the Marxian framework by going in other directions. In 1902 (the same year Lenin wrote *What Is To be Done?*), Georges Sorel (1847–1922) – a retired engineer in France who had started a second career in radical theorizing – had already started moving away from the ardent determinism of Marx's theories, focusing instead on how willed action and irrational drives motivate change.[25] By 1908, Sorel had turned away from orthodox Marxism and wrote his *Reflections on Violence*,[26] which emphasized the role of "myth" in political action. He used the example of the "General Strike," which was a term often used during this period to refer to the sought-after future social revolution that would destroy the class-based society. Sorel calls this a "myth," not in the sense of saying it is false, but rather to note that whether it is true or false is irrelevant – that masses of people *believe* it is true and are motivated to act on the basis of this belief, and that is what really matters. In his view, the masses rarely think through major issues, and instead are driven by myth, habit, and other irrational elements. In his view, for effective political change to happen these irrational elements must be taken into account. Sorel's views paralleled some parts of Lenin's thought, and would be one of the influences on Mussolini's view of politics.[27]

Finally, we turn to another revisionist who would become an important political figure later on: Benito Mussolini (1883–1945). In 1910, he began writing more for the socialist press in Italy, garnering a reputation as one of the best Marxist thinkers of the country.[28] In 1911, he would become the editor for *Avanti!*, the main socialist newspaper in the country. As time went on, and especially with the arrival of the First World War, Mussolini began to advocate for Italian involvement in the war rather than neutrality. This would result in his ouster from the Italian Socialist Party in 1914, and his explicit statements that Marx was wrong: that the nation – as a collective identity – was not "obsolete" (as in Marxist theory), but was the more important identification in this period. As he would frame the issue, the main struggle of the current period was between "proletarian nations" (such as Italy) against "plutocratic nations" (particularly the British and the United States). He would join the war as a soldier in 1915.

This brings us to the First World War itself. As discussed in Chapter 3, it seems that totalitarian movements rarely can gain political power unless some major crisis (or rather, group of crises) destabilize an area. It is hard to top the First World War as an instance of such a crisis. It also created substantial crises for the Marxian social democratic movement in two main ways. First, the ideology of the Second International (and many other Marxian-inspired groups) was that the proletariat of all nations had more in common with each other than any had with their own national bourgeois and capitalist classes. Therefore, the workers would not fight "the capitalists' war," but would instead join together in proletarian fraternity against the capitalist system itself. The war would then be the start of the "glorious workers' revolution" that Marx envisioned. However, it became clear very quickly that the workers did indeed feel kinship with their own nations and had few qualms at all about killing their "fraternal" workers in other countries (and in large numbers). It was the second problem, however, that created more substantial schisms. While the workers (uneducated, misled by the ruling class, and so on) might not understand their "true interests" in not fighting the war, surely the

Social Democratic parties would reject such chauvinistic national-ism, yes? Here, too, reality was far different from theory. Within the German parliament, the German Social Democratic Party, led by Kautsky, voted for war credits for the country, effectively signaling the Party's support for the war. It is hard to convey just how jarring this vote would be to the Marxists and others at the time. Lenin him-self viewed the vote as illustrating just how far the Second Interna-tional and the Western European social democratic parties had fallen from "true" Marxism.[29] It was from the multilevel chaos of the First World War that the new age of totalitarianism would grow.

The "Golden Age" of Totalitarianism

The first half of the twentieth century – particularly the period from 1917 until about 1953 – represents what one could call the "Golden Age" of totalitarianism. This is the period in which the major totali-tarian regimes appear – the Soviet Union (especially under Stalin), Fascist Italy, and Nazi Germany – while also being the origin point for later totalitarian regimes, such as East Germany, Albania, North Korea, and the People's Republic of China. It was during these years that totalitarianism not only held its greatest level of strength militar-ily and economically, but also when it gave the strongest impression as the "next stage" in human society – as the inevitable successor of "obsolete" parliamentary, liberal representative systems. During the "Golden Age" of totalitarianism, this mentality of inevitability also gave these regimes a certain level of legitimacy. If their opponents thought totalitarian victory was inescapable, was it not better to join with the "winning team" rather than being crushed by the "Right Side of History"?

It is important to start with the aftermath of the First World War. Beyond the sheer number of dead, the international system of Europe was fundamentally shattered.[30] Germany lost territory and the mon-archy was replaced with a new constitutional system (the Weimar Republic). The Austro-Hungarian Empire and Ottoman Empire ceased to exist, with a multitude of new nations in their places. The United States now took on a prominent role in European, and global, politics. For most nations involved in the conflict, there were significant internal changes as well. The First World War is usually considered the first major "total war," where all parts of society (be it the political, economic, or social spheres) were mobilized toward the goal of military victory, resulting in substantial centralization within national governments as well as an emphasis on regulation and planning (especially of the economy). Residents of these countries experienced much greater interference by government in their day-to-day lives, be it in government plans for factory production, rationing of food and goods, or incessant propaganda in various print media as well as in the newer forms of mass communication. Moreover, those fighting in the war often were scarred – physically and mentally – from the new and horrific style of war. In terms of future leaders, Mussolini's experience in the war helped form his views of a "trenchocracy," while Adolf Hitler spent the last part of the war hospitalized after suffering severe injuries due to a mustard gas attack. In ways both wonderous and frightening, the world after the war looked like a very different place than it was before the conflict. For our purposes, one of the most important transformations occurred when Tsarist Russia – long viewed as the main supporter of "reactionary" politics, be it through spearheading international groupings like the "Holy Alliance" or in the ongoing efforts (at home and abroad) of its secret police, the Okhrana – was toppled and replaced with the first Communist government to gain power.

The "October Revolution" occurred on 7 November (25 October in the "Old Style," or "OS," calendar used in Russia at that time) 1917, but we need to look a little earlier in that same year to see how this situation developed. Many countries suffered internal unrest during the war, but Tsarist Russia – already tenuous in its control – was especially unstable. The "February Revolution," which resulted in Tsar Nicholas II losing power and a "Provisional Government" being put in charge of Russia, started on 8 March (23 February "OS") 1917. Along with the issue of what new government should exist in Russia, the most pressing problem for the new government was the war. Should Russia continue fighting? Should it sue for peace and, if so, on what terms? What role, if any, should the Tsar (or monarchy in general) play in the new political order? The Provisional Government, first led by Prince Georgy Lvov but then by former Socialist-Revolutionary Party member Alexander Kerensky, continued on with the war. Tensions were high in Russia, and Lenin (at that point, living in Switzerland) saw as the opportunity for revolution. With aid from the German government, Lenin returned to Russia to mobilize the Bolsheviks in the country. The "October Revolution" was the result.

The Bolshevik Party quickly worked to consolidate its power. Obviously, there were more than a few people who were not pleased with the idea of a Communist government. Those designated "Class Enemies" by the Bolsheviks – who officially changed their name to the "Russian Communist Party (Bolshevik)" in 1918 – were not thrilled with the change: aristocrats, capitalists, the bourgeoisie, and the like. But other populations, especially the peasantry, were wary of the Communists as well. Besides the emphasis on the proletariat over the peasantry (and the not-infrequent writings from others, including Lenin himself, that peasants were at best untrustworthy and temporary allies), the peasantry also found the militant atheism of the Communists horrifying (made all the worse with persecution against religion, the burning of churches, and the torture/murder of clergy members and those in religious orders). All of these factors bring us to the Russian Civil War (1917–1923), with the primary contestants being the new Communist government (the "Reds") and the more diffuse group of loyalists to the Tsar and/or the previous constitutional government (usually called the "Whites"). It is also during this period that Lenin advanced what would later be called "war communism," which attempted to radically change Russia in short order and included the "militarization of labor," early workcamp prisons, major rationing, and severe forms of discipline for workers, among other things. It would be the first instance of fully totalitarian activity in the Communist regime, but not the last.[31]

The events in Russia had a galvanizing influence on other parts of Europe and the world. In the aftermath of the "October Revolution," multiple Communist parties were founded in various countries of Europe, Asia, and Latin America, including the Chinese Communist Party. Assisting these parties was the "Third International," better known as "Comintern," which was formed by Lenin in 1919 to push for Communism across the globe.[32] Moreover, other countries also saw possible radical coup attempts at this time. Some of these influences were directly from Communist Russia itself, such as Lenin's ill-fated attempt at invading Polish territory in 1919. But in most other places, it was the idea of the Communist revolution and its success that had the greatest effect. Some of the most immediate emulators were seen in Eastern and Central Europe, where governmental instability in various countries permitted greater influence or control by Communists, with the primary example being the "Hungarian Soviet Republic" in 1919 under Béla Kun. Similarly, attempts at forming new "Soviets" occurred in recently defeated Germany. The most famous (or perhaps notorious) example was the Bavarian Soviet Republic (1919).[33] It is also with the Bavarian Republic that we see the negative responses to the Communist revolution. In the case of Germany, the end of the war saw a significant number of veteran groups (*Freikorps*) maintaining their weapons on the idea that these veterans would "defend the nation" from foreign outsiders as much as possible.[34] For them, the spread of Communist ideology – especially in its Leninist form – presented a clear threat to the nation. It would be *Freikorps* units that would brutally put an end to the Bavarian Soviet Republic, which would be a good preview of the types of inter-totalitarian violence that would occur throughout the "Golden Age," be it in internal conflicts (like the Spanish Civil War) or international wars (such as the absolutely bloody clashes between Nazi Germany and Stalinist Soviet Union).[35]

The repercussions of the war and the Communist overthrow of Russia would also resonate in Italy. While the Russian Civil War raged on and the various groups in Germany battled, Italy had struggles as well. Although Italy was on the winning side of the First World War, many Italians believed that the country was cheated out of certain territorial concessions. Tensions were rampant in the country between a cacophony of political movements and groups, including syndicalists, anarchists, communists, monarchists, army veterans, criminal groups, and others. In the aftermath of the war, Mussolini began advocating for a "trenchocracy." In other words, rule by those who had sacrificed for the nation through their military service. Mussolini began organizing his Fascist combat squads in 1919, and a major activity for the organization was its violent actions against similarly violent leftwing extremists in various parts of Italy. Eventually forming the Fascists into a political party, Mussolini and the Fascists made their "March on Rome" on 27–29 October 1922, at which time Mussolini was appointed to the Prime Minister position by the King of Italy (Victor Emmanuel III).

In Germany, political violence between extremes on the Right and the Left continued. Among the groups that existed at this time were the "German Workers' Party" (or "DAP"), a nationalist anti-capitalist, but also anti-Marxist, group. Hitler (still in the military) was ordered to act as an intelligence and influence agent in the group. However, Hitler rose rather quickly in the party, and upon his discharge from the military in 1920, he moved into a permanent position within the party, which had recently been renamed the "National Socialist German Workers' Party" ("NSDAP," or Nazi party). Somewhat inspired by the March on Rome as well as by their own ideology, the Nazis under Hitler decided to attempt an overthrow of Bavaria in what is now known as the "Beer Hall Putsch" on 8 November 1923. The attempted insurrection was a disaster due to many factors. In the end, Hitler and others involved in the Putsch were arrested by the authorities.[36]

In some ways, we can consider 1924 as a key year in setting the stage for the totalitarian regimes of the Second World War. Early in the year (on 21 January), Lenin died after a period of illness and diminished capacity. The Communist Party's "Politburo" was the ruler of Soviet Russia, but Lenin had remained its main leader and focus of popular adoration. Lenin's death led to a period of ambiguity in terms of Communist leadership, as a mixture of ideological disputes and personal differences led to a division between two general tendencies (for lack of a better word). One tendency was led by Lev Bronstein (1879–1940), better known as Leon Trotsky. Highly intelligent and a fiery speaker, but also very confident in his own importance (to put it mildly), Trotsky had a talent for inspiring steadfast loyalty or implacable enmity from others.[37] The other tendency followed Ioseb Jughashvili (1878–1953), known to history as Joseph Stalin. A hardnosed man, Stalin was adept at ensuring that personnel with loyalty (and dependence) upon him were placed in many parts of the Soviet bureaucracy.[38] The midpart of the year saw changes in Italy. Although Mussolini had gained control of the country in 1922, his ability to fully transform the country in a Fascist direction was limited by other centers of power that still existed in the Parliament and government. The first major crisis of his rule occurred on 10 June, when Giacomo Matteotti (a Socialist member of parliament and ardent critic of Mussolini) was murdered by individuals supportive of the Fascist ideology. The end result of this crisis comes with a speech by Mussolini on 3 January 1925, which effectively begins the true start of the Fascist dictatorship in

Italy. Following the failed "Beer Hall Putsch," Hitler is sentenced (on 1 April) to five years' imprisonment for his actions, although he served only a fraction of this time, being pardoned and released later that year. It is during this time, however, that Hitler begins writing his *Mein Kampf* (translated as *My Struggle*, and first published in 1925),[39] and after his release confirms his position as the unquestioned leader of the Nazi Party. At this point, Hitler pushes for greater involvement of the Nazi party in electoral politics.

Other types of movements also begin to appear in this period that did not easily fit into communist, Fascist, or Nazi categories, and many of which would not gain greater success until later. In 1928, for instance, the Muslim Brotherhood was founded in Egypt by Hassan al-Banna,[40] and Abdul al-Maududi would start Jamaat-e-Islami in Lahore in 1941. These Islamic-focused organizations would not gain political power in this period, although various Islamic-oriented groups and polities would have some alliances with various totalitarian states in this period, including Nazi Germany.[41]

It is during this time that Stalin's control becomes more prominent.[42] The ideological and power struggle between Trotsky's and Stalin's factions continued for years, until Trotsky himself was thrown out of the USSR in 1929, with Stalin in a strong position to act. And act he did, strengthening the totalitarian apparatus within the Soviet Union. One of the major results was the attempt to "collectivize" agriculture in 1932, using brutal coercion and terror to bring about this change. The result was that millions were murdered through famine (most severely within Ukraine, but also elsewhere in the USSR) in what would later be called the "Terror Famine," or "Holodomor."[43] This event also gives a good example of the "winking" at excesses that would occur with various totalitarian regimes. Among others, a foreign correspondent for the *New York Times* (Walter Duranty) regularly downplayed the severity of the disaster during the famine.

While the Terror Famine raged in the Soviet Union during 1932–1933, politics remained tense in Germany. Suffering severely from the Great Depression, two major extremist parties in Germany benefited the most, both in terms of popularity and electoral success: the Nazi Party and the German Communist Party. The ongoing sclerosis of the national government and the increased tendency of the German Chancellor to use emergency powers to create regulations created political problems that aggravated the social fragility of the Weimar Republic. Having made significant gains in the national parliament, the Nazis – and Hitler in particular – became major figures in German politics. In early 1933, by a rather convoluted path, Hitler is appointed Chancellor of Germany. A mere month later, the German parliament building (*Reichstag*) is set on fire, and Hitler initially uses emergency powers to respond to the "threat," with many individuals from other political groups arrested. Soon after, the "Enabling Act" is passed that effectively ends the Weimar Republic and begins the Nazi regime. Nazi control of the government would continue growing, which included the founding of the Secret State Police (better known as the Gestapo) in 1933.

It is in 1934 that a tendency within totalitarian regimes showed itself clearly: the internal "purge" of party members. In mid-1934, Hitler permits the "Night of the Long Knives," where numerous members of the Nazi party's "Stormtroopers" (SA) were murdered, including Ernst Röhm. It is of particular note that Hitler and the Nazi party, now in full command of Germany, do not try to hide the murders, but instead justify their actions, using their dominance over media and government to amplify their position. Meanwhile, in the USSR, Sergei Kirov – a member of the Soviet Politburo and an up-and-coming member of the Party – was assassinated in Leningrad at the end of 1934. In the following years, the investigation of Kirov's murder would be the initial foundation for Stalin's "Great Purge." While Fascist Italy does not engage in similar murders within itself, it does embark on its brutal invasion of Abyssinia (now Ethiopia) in 1935.

During these last years before the Second World War, the full force of totalitarian rule became more dominant. While preparing the German war machine to extend into Europe, the Nazi regime also undertook major eugenic projects, including sterilizing thousands of the "unfit" and killing thousands of sickly individuals and children (considered "*Lenbensunwertes Leben*," or "life unworthy of life") through the *Aktion T4* program, which moved into the overall campaign to exterminate the "parasitic" Jewish race and other "inferior" races in the Holocaust.[44] In the Soviet Union, the "Great Purge" continued, with numerous arrests, millions sent to labor camps (or "Gulags"[45]), and many others executed, most notoriously including former Politburo members during various show trials in the late 1930s.[46] With the coming of the war, much of this brutality would also be directed by these totalitarian regimes against one another.

For our purposes, this chapter will not delve into the specifics of the Second World War. There are numerous histories, both academic and popularized, that provide good overviews of the conflict. We can simply note the destruction of the Nazi and Fascist regimes, and the formation of the "Western" bloc of representative democracies and the "Eastern" bloc of the Soviet Union and the Eastern European countries it conquered during the war.

Totalitarianism After the "Golden Age"

As the popular imagination usually sees Nazi Germany as the pinnacle of totalitarianism, its defeat is often viewed as the main endpoint in crushing totalitarian regimes. If that's the case, why do I put the end of the "Golden Era" eight years after the end of the Second World War? It is true that the year 1945 saw the final defeat of the Axis powers, but it did not signal the end of the totalitarian regimes of that era. The Soviet Union still remained, and its most explicitly totalitarian period would not end until Stalin's death on 5 March 1953. However, the end of the Second World War was not unimportant for totalitarianism. The end of the war smashed the overarching sensation and fear that totalitarianism of one form or another was inevitable, although there was the sense that one form of it (the Communist variant) might still be inevitable.

After Stalin's death, the USSR began moving in a post-totalitarian direction, exemplified by the "Secret Speech" of 1956 that admitted some of the crimes of the "Great Purge" as well as directly blaming them on Stalin himself. Between this acknowledgement and some of the brutal repressions by the Soviets in Eastern European countries, much of the allure of the Soviet Union lessened for radicals in this period. Many of them would instead turn to a new "shining" example of communism: China under Mao. Part of the attraction of Mao to various totalitarians of this period was the lack of "excesses" (a euphemism often used for atrocities) that occurred under Stalin. But, as with Stalin, this view required a large amount of willful ignoring of activities in China. By 1958, Mao's regime had already begun the "Great Leap Forward," a campaign similar to the Soviet agricultural "collectivization" process, but with even more horrific results. Over a period of about four years, tens of millions were starved to death by famine in China.[47] Later on, starting in 1966, Mao initiated the "Cultural Revolution," a period of severe repression, unending surveillance, and mass fanaticism.[48] Alas, various radicals saw the Cultural Revolution not as a totalitarian nightmare, but as an inspiration. But another part of the attraction was the non-Western nature of the Chinese Communist Party and Mao himself.

Mao's non-Western and anti-imperialist appearance was popular insofar as this was also the period in which decolonization became a dominant feature on the international scene. As this process was often conflictual, instability provided avenues for totalitarian ideologies and movements to flourish, especially as possible fringe groups in larger "national liberation" movements. Categorization of totalitarian types becomes tricky in this period. In the broadest sense, one could say that leftwing forms of totalitarian ideology and organization dominated, reflected in the self-identification of these groups as part of the Left, the frequent use of Marxist (or at least Marxian) language, as well as through the positive references to Lenin (especially his *Imperialism: The Highest Stage of Capitalism*[49]), Fidel Castro, Che Guevara, and Mao (among others). But the situation is a little more complicated. Various "national liberation" movements (both in language and in practice) show striking similarities to Italian Fascism, but none of them explicitly align with that ideology (and, instead, often accuse their opponents of fascism). While Marxism often served as the language of radicalism (and as a source of self-identification), the practice tended to follow more fascistic, or even just authoritarian, directions.

This is also the period of "New Left" terrorism in Western Europe and North America (among other places). In contrast to the "national liberation" movements in the developing world, none of these New Left organizations managed to overthrow a Western government by force. That said, it is prudent to recall the concern from Chapter 3: as none of these groups managed to gain power, can we call them totalitarian? Their ideologies – and their internal organization – do seem to make that reasonable. All of them emphasized notions along the lines of directional "History," and these groups were particularly focused upon "world-historic" populations. While many of them still used Marxian language, however, a distinguishing feature of "New Left" totalitarians was their disenchantment with the earlier "world-historic" population. As the actual working class (rather than the exalted "Proletariat" of earlier Marxists) had shown itself quite content with decent pay and reasonable working hours instead of demanding social revolution and the "classless society," the "New Left" extremists sought out new "savior" classes, for lack of a better phrase. Various subpopulations became the new "world-historic" populace, including racial minorities, women, formerly colonized people, sexual minorities, linguistic minorities, and many others. Organizationally, many of the "New Left" radicals did not seek to become mass political parties, but rather viewed themselves as "precursor" groups. Viewing themselves as under severe constraints – which, to a certain extent was true, as the experiences with pre-Second World War extremist organizations had made Western societies and security forces much more aware of the possibility that such groups could take power – these New Left associations instead considered "raising the consciousness" of the population as their main task, with a mass political party arising later on. A typical formulation was that these smaller groups would act as the "spark" that would start a revolutionary "fire" among the "world-historic" populations, which would then lead to mass organizing, social revolution, and the "New Society." Among the various groups in this period, the most well-organized included the Weather Underground Organization (WUO) in the United States[50] and the Red Army Faction (also known as the "Baader-Meinhof Gang") in West Germany,[51] while other groups – such as Jim Jones' "Peoples' Temple"[52] as well as the Symbionese Liberation Army[53] – blurred the line between totalitarian radicalism, simple criminality, and cult-like organization. There are also some "borderline" organizations that straddle the line between "New Left" and "national liberation," at least in their own minds. The best example of such a group is the Black Panther Party of the United States,[54] which aligned with various New Left groups (and was often praised by the WUO and other such groups) but also viewed itself as a colonized people (specifically, Black Americans) seeking "liberation" from "imperialist" masters.

A different type of totalitarianism in this period is based on religion. Unlike the "New Left" forms, these religious totalitarian organizations did, on occasion, manage to take political power. Although the Islamist[55] totalitarian ideologies have their origins in the early

1900s, their level of influence was middling until about the late 1970s. Before that time, most of the "space" for these types of movements were taken up by Marxist/Communist ideologies and nationalist (especially "pan-Arabic") movements. The one exception to this trend would be the Kingdom of Saudi Arabia, which has based some of its legitimacy upon its adherence to Salafism. However, here again we encounter the problem of whether such a system is totalitarian in nature or more similar to earlier, pre-modern forms of regimes. It is in the late 1970s that two major events occurred and brought Islamism (in its various forms) to greater attention: the Islamic Revolution in Iran beginning in 1978 (culminating in the formation of the Islamic Republic of Iran under Ayatollah Ruhollah Khomeini)[56] and the assassination of Egyptian President Anwar Sadat in Egypt by Muslim Brotherhood members in 1981. These events illustrated the increased vitality of Islamist extremism and totalitarianism and helped inspire other types of Islamists to take action. The creation of Al-Qaeda in 1988 marks a major shift for Islamism, moving from a more regional focus (primarily in the Middle East) to an international focus. While causing a great deal of damage and managing to ally with the Taliban of Afghanistan, Al-Qaeda lacked the ability to gain greater political control in other areas. As noted in Chapter 3, totalitarian movements and organizations have greater success during periods of crisis and war. This trend remains true for Islamists, as illustrated in the case of the "Islamic State," also known as ISIS and ISIL.[57] The chaos that ensued after the American invasion of Iraq in 2003, and aggravated by the start of the Syrian Civil War in 2011, created a vacuum of legitimacy and order that permitted the Islamic State to gain control and begin its destruction of those deemed idolatrous or lacking in fidelity. While the militaries of multiple countries managed to weaken the Islamic State severely, it is possible that some similar type of regime could come to power again.

Conclusion

We finally come to the present in our history and consider where totalitarianism stands now. A major difficulty in trying to see if there are emerging and/or new forms of totalitarianism today is a language problem. As mentioned in Chapter 1, "totalitarianism" is a word that is often loosely used, and frequently serves as a rhetorical weapon to describe something that is disliked. That being said, however, it is not unwarranted to consider some disquieting trends in recent years. We will consider some of these trends in the next chapter.

Summing Up

- Major ideological and organizational developments occurred in the mid-1700s through late 1800s that would form the "infrastructure" of totalitarianism, with the "Reign of Terror" in the French Revolution as the first "proto-totalitarian" regime to exist.
- It is in the period near the end of the First World War until the early 1950s that totalitarianism had its "Golden Age" – an era where it seemed as if totalitarian regimes (be they based on class, nation, or race) were the "way of the future."
- Following the Second World War and the death of Stalin, totalitarian ideologies tended to shift toward different "subaltern" types of populations as well as toward religion, and totalitarian organizations had less success in holding political power for extended periods of time.

Suggested Reading

Thus far, there is no singular text on the history of totalitarianism. However, there are numerous books and articles that focus on particular movements, historical periods, regimes, leaders, ideologies, and the like. The texts referenced in this chapter will provide the reader with some good places to start, and each of these works have well-developed bibliographies. If the reader is interested in some broader historical texts, consider some of the following works. On Communism, Service (2007) provides a good overview, with some other details provided by Brown (2009). For Italian Fascism, Payne (1995) is by far the best and most accessible text. For those interested in a general history of Nazism, give Burleigh (2000) an examination. For Mao's reign in China, the trilogy of works by Dikötter (2016, 2013, 2010) would be most useful. While limited to only two groups on the "New Left," the overview by Varon (2004) gives a good feel for the era.

Notes

1. Cohn (1970).
2. Moreover, there is a tendency to view the medieval period as one extended exercise in oppression and despotism, especially in the realm of ideas. This is a rather large oversimplification. For a better view, see Nederman (2000).
3. For more on this period, see Watt (2020).
4. See Hill (1975), among others.
5. For some discussion along these lines, see Melzer (1990) and Miller (1984).
6. For instance, see Yack (1992) and Talmon (1985).
7. Rousseau (1984).
8. Rousseau (1994).
9. For instance, see Tackett (2015).
10. For a good general overview of the French Revolution, see Doyle (2018) and McPhee (2016). On the Jacobins and their rule, see Palmer (2005). Also see Robespierre (2007).
11. Consider the discussion in Hunt and Censer (2017).
12. For a broad, yet interesting history of Europe in the period between the Napoleonic Wars and the First World War, see Evans (2016).
13. Dawson (2010): 47.
14. While it is always good for the reader to examine the original works of writers themselves, Hegel's works are far from accessible, even for people with training in philosophy. For readers interested in his views on politics and the state, Avineri (1972) provides a welcome clarity to Hegel's thought.
15. Feuerbach (1989).
16. For an excellent and accessible text that covers both Marx's life and his ideas, see Sperber (2013).
17. See Sperber (2005).
18. Marx's writings are voluminous, and many of them can be a mixture of dense and tedious. A good group of selections can be found in Marx (1978). Additionally, Avineri (1968) and Tucker (1969) give good overviews of his general thought as it would relate to our topic.
19. Jensen (2014): 32
20. Pauli (2015): 68–72.
21. Gray (2020).
22. Gregor (2009).
23. Among others, see Harding (2009), Service (1985) and Meyer (1957).
24. Lenin (1969[1902]).
25. Ohana (2009); Horowitz (1961).
26. Sorel (2004[1950]).
27. See Sternhell (1994) for a good overview of these influences and developments.
28. See Bosworth (2010); Hibbert (2008).
29. Nation (2009).
30. A comprehensive overview of the war can be found in Gilbert (1994).
31. With some qualifications, a very good overview of this period is Pipes (1990).

32. See Hallas (2008), but with qualifications. See also Firsoc, Klehr, and Haynes (2014).
33. For a rather sympathetic discussion of the Bavarian Republic, see Harman (2003).
34. On this event and numerous others, see Schumann (2009).
35. For an interesting overview that puts most of the first half of the twentieth century in context, see Payne (2011).
36. While a biography of Hitler himself, Kershaw (1998) is a most accessible source on these early days of the Nazi party.
37. Service (2009).
38. For an interesting analysis, see Van Ree (2002).
39. Hitler (1999[1927]).
40. Mitchell (1969).
41. Motadel (2014).
42. For a quite readable overview of Stalin's life as ruler of the Soviet Union, see Montefiore (2003).
43. The best source remains Conquest (1986).
44. Burleigh and Wipperman (1991).
45. Applebaum (2003).
46. Conquest (2008).
47. Yang (2012).
48. MacFarquhar and Schoenhals (2006).
49. Lenin (1987[1917]).
50. Jacobs (1997).
51. Smith and Moncourt (2009, 2013).
52. Scheeres (2012).
53. Symbionese Liberation Army (2019).
54. Bloom and Martin (2013). See also Newton (2009).
55. See Mozaffari (2017); Maher (2016).
56. See Axworthy (2013); and also Nasr (2006).
57. Among others, see Warrick (2016) as well as Lister (2015).

Bibliography

Applebaum, Anne. 2003. *Gulag: A History*. New York: Anchor Books.

Avineri, Shlomo. 1968. *The Social and Political Thought of Karl Marx*. Cambridge: Cambridge University Press.

Avineri, Shlomo. 1972. *Hegel's Theory of the Modern State*. Cambridge: Cambridge University Press.

Axworthy, Michael. 2013. *Revolutionary Iran: A History of the Islamic Republic*. Oxford: Oxford University Press.

Bloom, Joshua, and Waldo E. Martin, Jr. 2013. *Black Against Empire: The History and Politics of the Black Panther Party*. Berkeley: University of California Press.

Bosworth, R. J. B. 2010. *Mussolini*. London: Bloomsbury.

Brown, Archie. 2009. *The Rise and Fall of Communism*. New York: Ecco.

Burleigh, Michael. 2000. *The Third Reich: A New History*. New York: Hill and Wang.

Burleigh, Michael, and Wolfgang Wipperman. 1991. *The Racial State: Germany 1933–1945*. Cambridge: Cambridge University Press.

Castro, Fidel. 2008. *The Declaration of Havana*. London: Verso.

Cohn, Norma. 1970. *The Pursuit of the Millennium: Revolutionary Millenarians and Mystical Anarchists of the Middle Ages*. New York: Oxford University Press.

Conquest, Robert. 1986. *The Harvest of Sorrow: Soviet Collectivization and the Terror-Famine*. New York: Oxford University Press.

Conquest, Robert. 2008. *The Great Terror: A Reassessment*. Fortieth Anniversary Edition. Oxford: Oxford University Press.

Dawson, Christopher. 2010. *The Crisis of Western Education*. Washington, DC: Catholic University Press of America.

Dikötter, Frank. 2010. *Mao's Great Famine: The History of China's Most Devastating Catastrophe, 1958–1962*. New York: Walker & Company.

Dikötter, Frank. 2013. *The Tragedy of Liberation: A History of the Chinese Revolution 1945–1957*. London: Bloomsbury.

Dikötter, Frank. 2016. *The Cultural Revolution: A People's 1962–1976*. London: Bloomsbury.

Doyle, William. 2018. *The Oxford History of the French Revolution*. Oxford: Oxford University Press.

Evans, Richard J. 2016. *The Pursuit of Power: Europe 1815–1914*. New York: Penguin Books.

Feuerbach, Ludwig. 1989. *The Essence of Christianity*. Buffalo: Prometheus Books.

Firsoc, Fridrish I., Harvey Klehr, and John Earl Haynes. 2014. *Secret Cables of the Comintern, 1933–1943*. Lynn Visson, trans. New Haven: Yale University Press.

Gilbert, Martin. 1994. *The First World War: A Complete History*. New York: Henry Holt and Company.

Gray, Phillip W. 2020. *Vanguardism: Ideology and Organization in Totalitarian Politics*. New York: Routledge.

Gregor, A. James. 2009. *Marxism, Fascism, and Totalitarianism: Chapters in the Intellectual History of Radicalism*. Stanford: Stanford University Press.

Hallas, Duncan. 2008. *The Comintern: A History of the Third International*. Chicago: Haymarket Press.

Harding, Neil. 2009. *Lenin's Political Thought*. Chicago: Haymarket Books.

Harman, Chris. 2003. *The Lost Revolution: Germany 1918 to 1923*. Chicago: Haymarket Press.

Hibbert, Christopher. 2008. *Mussolini: The Rise and Fall of Il Duce*. New York: St. Martin's Press.

Hill, Christopher. 1975. *The World Turned Upside Down: Radical Ideas during the English Revolution*. New York: Penguin Books.

Hitler, Adolf. 1999[1927]. *Mein Kampf*. Ralph Manheim, trans. Boston: Mariner Books.

Horowitz, Irving Louis. 1961. *Radicalism and the Revolt against Reason: The Social Theories of Georges Sorel with a Translation of His Essay on "the Decomposition of Marxism"*. London: Routledge.

Hunt, Lynn, and Jack R. Censer. 2017. *The French Revolution and Napoleon: Crucible of the Modern World*. London: Bloomsbury Academic.

Jacobs, Ron. 1997. *The Way the Wind Blew: A History of the Weather Underground*. London: Verso.

Jensen, Richard Bach. 2014. *The Battle against Anarchist Terrorism: An International History, 1878–1934*. Cambridge: Cambridge University Press.

Kershaw, Ian. 1998. *Hitler: 1889–1936: Hubris*. New York: W.W. Norton & Company.

Lenin, V. I. 1969[1902]. *What Is To Be Done? Burning Questions of Our Movement*. New York: International Publishers.

Lenin, V. I. 1987[1917]. "Imperialism: The Highest Stage of Capitalism." In H. M. Christman (ed.), *Essential Works of Lenin: "What Is to Be Done?" and Other Writings*. New York: Dover Publications, pp. 178–270.

Lister, Charles R. 2015. *The Syrian Jihad: Al-Qaeda, the Islamic State and the Evolution of an Insurgency*. Oxford: Oxford University Press.

MacFarquhar, Roderick, and Michael Schoenhals. 2006. *Mao's Last Revolution*. Cambridge: Belknap Press.

Maher, Shiraz. 2016. *Salafi-Jihadism: The History of an Idea*. Oxford: Oxford University Press.

Marx, Karl. 1978. *The Marx-Engels Reader*. Robert C. Tucker, ed. Second Edition. New York: W. W. Norton & Company.

McPhee, Peter. 2016. *Liberty or Death: The French Revolution*. New Haven: Yale University Press.

Melzer, Arthur M. 1990. *The Natural Goodness of Man: On the System of Rousseau's Thought*. Chicago: University of Chicago Press.

Meyer, Alfred G. 1957. *Leninism*. New York: Frederick A. Praeger.

Miller, James. 1984. *Rousseau: Dreamer of Democracy*. New Haven: Yale University Press.

Mitchell, Richard P. 1969. *The Society of Muslim Brothers*. Oxford: Oxford University Press.

Montefiore, Simon Sebag. 2003. *Stalin: The Court of the Red Tsar*. New York: Vintage Books.

Motadel, David. 2014. *Islam and Nazi Germany's War*. Cambridge: Belknap Press.

Mozaffari, Mehdi. 2017. *Islamism: A New Totalitarianism*. Boulder: Lynne Rienner Publishers.

Nasr, Vali. 2006. *The Shia Revival: How Conflicts within Islam will Shape the Future.* New York: W. W. Norton & Company.

Nation, R. Craig. 2009. *War on War: Lenin, the Zimmerwald Left, and the Origins of the Communist International.* Chicago: Haymarket Books.

Nederman, Cary J. 2000. *Worlds of Difference: European Discourses on Toleration, c. 1100–1550.* University Park: Pennsylvania State University Press.

Newton, Huey P. 2009. *To Die for the People: The Writings of Huey P. Newton.* Toni Morrison, ed. San Francisco: City Lights Books.

Ohana, David. 2009. *The Dawn of Political Nihilism: Volume I of the Nihilist Order.* Brighton: Sussex Academic Press.

Palmer, R. R. 2005. *Twelve Who Ruled: The Year of Terror in the French Revolution.* Princeton: Princeton University Press.

Pauli, Benjamin J. 2015. "Pacifism, Nonviolence, and the Reinvention of Anarchist Tactics in the Twentieth Century." *Journal of the Study of Radicalism* 9(1): 61–94.

Payne, Stanley G. 1995. *A History of Fascism, 1914–1945.* Madison: University of Wisconsin Press.

Payne, Stanley G. 2011. *Civil War in Europe, 1905–1949.* Cambridge: Cambridge University Press.

Pipes, Richard. 1990. *The Russian Revolution.* New York: Vintage Books.

Robespierre, Maximilien. 2007. *Virtue and Terror.* Jean Ducange, ed. London: Verso.

Rousseau, Jean-Jacques. 1984. *A Discourse on Inequality.* New York: Penguin Books.

Rousseau, Jean-Jacques. 1994. *The Social Contract.* Oxford: Oxford University Press.

Scheeres, Julia. 2012. *A Thousand Lives: The Untold Story of Jonestown.* New York: Free Press.

Schumann, Dirk. 2009. *Political Violence in the Weimar Republic, 1918–1933: Fight for the Streets and Fear of Civil War.* Thomas Dunlap, trans. New York: Berghahn Books.

Service, Robert. 1985. *Lenin: A Political Life: Volume I: The Strengths of Contradiction.* Bloomington: Indiana University Press.

Service, Robert. 2007. *Comrades! A History of World Communism.* Cambridge: Harvard University Press.

Service, Robert. 2009. *Trotsky: A Biography.* Cambridge: Belknap Press.

Smith, J., and Andre Moncourt. 2009. *The Red Army Faction: A Documentary History: Volume I: Projectiles for the People.* Oakland: PM Press.

Smith, J., and Andre Moncourt. 2013. *The Red Army Faction: A Documentary History: Volume II: Dancing with Imperialism.* Oakland: PM Press.

Sorel, Georges. 2004[1950]. *Reflections on Violence.* T. E. Hulme and J. Roth, trans. Mineola: Dover Publications, Inc.

Sperber, Jonathan. 2005. *The European Revolutions, 1848–1851.* Cambridge: Cambridge University Press.

Sperber, Jonathan. 2013. *Karl Marx: A Nineteenth-Century Life.* New York: Liveright Publishing Corporation.

Sternhell, Zeev. 1994. *The Birth of Fascist Ideology: From Cultural Rebellion to Political Revolution.* David Maisel, trans. Princeton: Princeton University Press.

Symbionese Liberation Army. 2019. *Death to the Fascist Insect.* John Brian King, ed. No Location: Spurl Editions.

Tackett, Timothy. 2015. *The Coming of the Terror in the French Revolution.* Cambridge: Belknap Press.

Talmon, J. L. 1985. *The Origins of Totalitarian Democracy.* Cambridge: Westview Press.

Tucker, Robert C. 1969. *The Marxian Revolutionary Idea.* New York: W. W. Norton & Company.

Van Ree, Erik. 2002. *The Political Thought of Joseph Stalin: A Study in Twentieth-Century Revolutionary Patriotism.* London: RoutledgeCurzon.

Varon, Jeremy. 2004. *Bringing the War Home: The Weather Underground, the Red Army Faction, and Revolutionary Violence in the Sixties and Seventies.* Berkeley: University of California Press.

Warrick, Joby. 2016. *Black Flags: The Rise of ISIS.* New York: Anchor Books.

Watt, Jeffrey R. 2020. *The Consistory and Social Discipline in Calvin's Geneva.* Rochester: University of Rochester.

Yack, Bernard. 1992. *The Longing for Total Revolution: Philosophic Sources of Social Discontent from Rousseau to Marx and Nietzsche.* Berkeley: University of California Press.

Yang, Jisheng. 2012. *Tombstone: The Great Chinese Famine 1958–1962.* New York: Farrar, Straus and Giroux.

6

THE FUTURE OF TOTALITARIANISM

There are few things that would be as unmitigated a blessing to humanity than for totalitarianism to be of merely historical interest – a horrible civilizational "wrong turn" with little contemporary or future relevance. Alas, we lack such a blessing. We will now turn to the future and consider what possible directions totalitarianism may take in the coming decades.

This chapter will be speculative, of course. While there is no shortage of people (especially those with university degrees) who think they can predict the future, tomorrow must always remain obscure. The future (if any) of totalitarianism is opaque as well. We can see many of the strands that led to totalitarian movements and regimes when we look back through history, but it is much harder to see these strands and dynamics when you are in the middle of them, rather than viewing them as past events. This problem is compounded by how people often think of totalitarianism. Most of us would like to believe that we would be the woman who refused to join the crowds giving the Roman salute as Hitler passed by, the man who would not join in abusing dissidents in a struggle session during Mao's Cultural Revolution, or the family who would hide Jews to save them from the Gestapo. It's a nice thought; a comforting thought. But it's a thought that often hinges on the idea that people in these regimes mostly acted from pure fear and/or animosity, and that people in these regimes believed that the ideologies animating these societies were wrong and evil. As noted throughout this book, much of the population in these places sincerely believed they were moving to a new and better society, and that destroying the "enemies" of the regime was a necessary step for this grand new era to begin. It's easy

DOI: 10.4324/9781003254232-6

to imagine oneself as part of the Resistance when the events are in the past, and there is a general social consensus about which side was right and which was wrong. It is much harder to be attentive to these issues in one's own time, in one's own society, and especially if a given movement or ideology might overlap with one's own notions of what is good and proper. So, in speculating about the future of totalitarianism, one thing we (the author included) must always consider is that the danger might not arise with "them" – "those people" who we see as a threat – but among "us," among "we decent, good people" and those who are allies with us.

Continuing Totalitarian Regimes

Despite the destruction of the Axis totalitarian regimes by 1945 and the collapse of the Soviet Union in 1991, at least one obviously totalitarian regime still exists: North Korea (the "Democratic People's Republic of Korea"), although some observers might include other regimes as well (such as Eritrea). An encouraging element about a regime like North Korea is that it is small and limited in their ability to expand. The nuclear program of the North Korean government presents challenges, of course, but except for a few fringe individuals and groups in the West, there is little appetite or resonance for the "*Juche*" ideology outside of territory under the control of the North Korean state itself.

That being said, there is one post-totalitarian country that presents a greater challenge. While the People's Republic of China (PRC) has decreased in its severity – in some ways – since the death of Mao in 1976, it has remained a significantly repressive country toward its own population and often indicates its desire to spread its control to areas near its territory. While one could also make similar claims about the Russian Federation – and its increasingly dictatorial rule under Vladimir Putin – a major difference between Russia and China is the substantial change in Russian government structures and ideology after the end of the Soviet Union versus the continuity that exists within China, even after Mao's death. The current Russian Federation is an authoritarian state with a developed security apparatus, but much of the previous totalitarian and post-totalitarian systems that had existed collapsed with the Soviet Union itself, and were replaced with a more oligarchic form of government. In contrast, there was no collapse after Mao's demise. While major changes arose under the rule of Deng Xiaoping (from 1978 to between 1989 to 1992), this was a change to a post-totalitarian system rather than a complete shift to an authoritarian one. Even more concerning is the reemergence of more explicitly totalitarian elements within the PRC's current leadership under Xi Jinping, who some observers fear may be seeking a revival of more Maoist-style forms of rule in solidifying his own position.

Unlike places such as North Korea, China does present a greater potential threat in three ways. First, China is a much larger and more powerful country. With a population estimated at nearly 1.5 billion people and a highly developed military, the PRC is a notable geopolitical force. Moreover, its economic power – as one of, if not the, main supplier for manufactured goods under the system of globalization – makes it a major strategic player in world economic affairs. Second, the Chinese government appears to be seeking to make economic and cultural inroads into various countries throughout the world, be it through mining interests in places like the Republic of Congo, its expansive "Belt and Road Initiative" in numerous countries, or the placement of numerous "Confucius Institutes" in Western universities. With its long cultural history and significant resources, China can spread its influence much more widely than many other states (totalitarian or otherwise). Third, a notable amount of people do look to the PRC's system as something worth emulating, even if only partially. Writers in major Western newspapers, some academics from major institutions, various Western government officials, and others have expressed interest or even admiration of parts of the PRC's system. One needs to only look at some of the various writings by Westerners on China's "success" in handling the COVID-19 pandemic as a recent example. This last point is perhaps the most concerning. In looking to the past, one of the more consistent mistakes from various "experts" and others was the belief that one could have the benefits of totalitarianism (efficiency, unity in purpose, and the like) without the negatives (crushing of rights, widespread misery, annihilation of others).[1] One might surmise that a big reason for this delusion is the assumption by these individuals that "good, decent" people like themselves would be in charge, and "of course" would not engage in such activities. At best, this is naïve.

Beyond the potential ideological changes in China are the technological advances that are of great concern. Categorizing Chinese subjects into good or bad groupings is a long-standing practice within the Communist regime, as is significant levels of surveillance. But it is the more insidious creation of a "social credit" system that may give us a glimpse of what a future totalitarian system would entail. Could technological developments assist in the creation of a totalitarianism that is more all-encompassing and pervasive than that of the past?

Technology and the Ease of Totalitarianism

There is often a connection, both in our minds as well as in reality, between totalitarianism and advanced forms of technology. While this can include mental images of columns of soldiers marching with missiles or tanks, there is also the ongoing images of huge screens with the leader's face, inescapable cameras everywhere, and the (well-founded) suspicion of listening equipment in places public and private. This is not merely a reflection of the types of films or novels that exist on totalitarianism. There are good, historical reasons for these views. When considering the totalitarian regimes of the past, most of the ones that managed to survive (beyond a few months) made significant use of the most recent technology available, especially technology involving mass communications, mass surveillance, and organizational tools – beyond military advancements.[2] Outside of areas where a totalitarian regime was particularly isolated – North Korea and Albania being the primary examples – these types of governments focused strongly on advancing certain forms of technology, even while their own subjects would be stuck with comparatively low technology in their day-to-day life.

One of the most striking changes of the last 40 years is the "telecommunications revolution." With advancements in numerous areas, as well as the spread of technology across society – where once computers were for offices (if even there), "beepers" were for medical doctors, and mobile phones were the toy of rich financiers, now average households have at least one computer, and large swaths of the global population keep miniature supercomputers in their pockets that often act primarily as internet and social media connection units and only secondarily as phones – the telecommunications revolution has radically changed society. Information travels faster, networks of people can interact instantly while thousands of miles apart, and computerized data can be analyzed with remarkable speed along numerous network nodes.

These changes can also influence totalitarian movements and parties. "Through the advancements of transportation and telecommunications technology and infrastructure, the extensive, costly, and immobile material infrastructure of parties/groups is now interconnected, more cost-efficient, and mobile. With these material changes come organizational changes."[3] Before and during the "Golden Age" of totalitarianism, a major role of totalitarian parties within movements was the creation of infrastructure: organizational "charts" so lines-of-command could develop, provision of printing presses for newspapers/pamphlets/flyers, financial repositories for collecting and distributing funds, and the like. While these types of arrangements were most useful in 1924, they are obviously rather more clunky now. In some ways, the telecommunications revolution is greatly beneficial, insofar as the spread of information may act to "diffuse" totalitarian movements/parties from gaining as much popularity. The increased ease of communication might also mean that totalitarian movements, parties, and sects are more likely to be undercut by some of their own deficiencies. Historically, many totalitarian parties and movements collapsed under their own internal disputes on topics that seem rather obscure. In a sense, the telecommunications revolution may act as a means of "quarantining" many of these movements, or at least many of those who would be inclined to join them. How many potential Lenins or Hitlers have, rather than focusing on building up organizations and movements, instead dedicated their time and energy to pointless "flame wars" and "trolling" on sites like Reddit, Twitter, or 4chan?

But, as with most things, there are negative aspects as well as positive ones to the telecommunications revolution. One aspect of this spread is polarization and "mainstreaming" of types of totalitarian thinking (discussed in greater detail in the next section). Another aspect is the increased ease, and increased intensity, of surveillance. Here we turn to the "social credit" system as an example. Consider how many types of online purchasing or social media operate. Dependent upon the user's actions, the system can extrapolate (based on large amounts of data) into what "niches" the user "fits." A person who clicks the "like" button on a Manchester United post would be put into a "niche" that also includes people who live in certain countries (such as Britain or India), people who purchase beer, and the like. A person who views a video from an ecologically focused company would likely be put in a "niche" of leaning left in political views, being in a middle-class or higher income bracket, and a subscriber to various streaming services. Now, imagine such a system, but for everything: every bank transaction, every post (on whatever medium) you write or like, every connection (direct or indirect) you have with others, and so forth, all being part of your "digital identity." The "credit" part is similar to a credit score in finance, where one's previous history (paying off loans on time versus going into default, number of accounts, and the like) strongly influences the likelihood of being able to get a mortgage or a car loan. "Social credit" means that one's choices could have wide ramifications. Using the earlier example, if you "like" Manchester United, your social credit score might go down (as the system considers such preferences to be unhealthy), which could limit the type of travel you could do or what types of purchase you can make. The unnerving question for a "social credit" system then becomes, "who decides?" Whoever decides what is "sociable" and what is "antisocial" effectively determines what can and cannot be done in a technologically advanced country. While earlier totalitarian systems had to rely upon microphones, cameras, and informants to spy on the population, today's integrated form of technology would allow such a regime to know every purchase you make on a debit card, every word you say near a smartphone, and every search you start when you say, "Hey Google." Whatever shape future totalitarian regimes might take, technological advancement would appear to make the job of curtailing resistance all the more easy for them.

The "Mainstreaming" of Totalitarian Ideology

Historically speaking, it seems rare for a regime to become totalitarian spontaneously or simply as a response to circumstances. Usually, a regime already has totalitarian ideologies/movements within it that gain full expression in response to opportunities. It's not as if a totalitarian government pops out, fully formed, from the head of the previous system, like Athena from Zeus (if you'll forgive the classical reference). Rather, the ideologies and movements that form the totalitarian system have been percolating (or perhaps "festering" would be a more appropriate term) to some degree over many years or decades. Almost any modern society – with perhaps the exceptions very small, isolated, and homogenous ones – will have various dissident ideas and populations within it, and obviously these are not all totalitarian or dangerous. Some (perhaps many) of them may indeed be beneficial. But among them can lie totalitarian ideologies and groups. As noted in Chapters 3 and 5, it is very easy for broader movements to "wink at" or excuse more extreme elements within them. This "winking at" totalitarian parts of the movement allows for "percolation." In some cases, the totalitarian components go nowhere and remain the obsession and eccentricities of a small number of people. But there are other cases where something much worse occurs: the styles of thinking, arguments, and/or organization of the totalitarian parts gain more prominence within the broader movements. This is a rather gradual process. Indeed, many of the broader proponents of a movement are not even aware that they are absorbing such totalitarian elements into their own thinking and (once again, from the inclination to "wink at" the more extreme elements) are not often interested in seeing how their own forms of thinking are being shaped by totalitarian viewpoints. It is this gradual process that one can call the "mainstreaming" of totalitarian ideology.

This mainstreaming of totalitarian forms of thinking[4] shows itself by taking on the categories, distinctions, and even the language of totalitarian ideology while not necessarily taking on the ideology fully. Let's try to clarify what that means. In Chapter 2, we briefly discussed ideology, and noted how most people have an ideology, but not one that is fully thought out. It is in the "mainstreaming" process that this lack of self-reflection on one's beliefs becomes precarious. The expansion of the styles of thinking are so gradual, and can go along similar "grooves" of thought or language, that many do not realize that the premises of their ideas are much more radical than they thought. A typical historical example that can be used is of Germany in the first part half of the twentieth century. The German Communist Party did not pop up out of nowhere, nor did the Nazi Party just appear one day to take control. In both cases, these organizations used ideas and language that had already "seeped into" broader discourse through the ongoing efforts of groups like the Social Democratic Party, the *Völkisch* movement, and others.[5] People who focused on the problems of the working-class or on the identity of the German nation slowly started thinking in terms of broader categories like "Proletariat" and "Aryan Race" because the most forceful articulations of these issues increasingly came from speakers/writers with totalitarian ideologies, while writers from other political tendencies lacked a way to present a clear, and concise response of their own.

For the purposes of illustration, we will focus on the West here (especially America) and use two broad strands of thought that reflect this "mainstreaming": what we could call the "Alt-Right" and the "Intersectional Left." These may be terms you have heard in other contexts. But keep in mind here that these two groups are "constructions" for discussion. It would be hard to say that there is any party or organization that is clearly "Alt-Right" or "Intersectional Left," much less that there is a straightforward or clear movement for either of them. Rather, these two names indicate broad ideological "tendencies" (for lack of a better phrase) that will hopefully give a better sense of how more unpleasant ideologies can "percolate" into more mainstream conversations.

Let's start with the one that may be more familiar from media reports, which would be the Alt-Right. For our purposes, the Alt-Right entails those who mainly focus on population dynamics, be it focused on race (especially in the American context) or "*ethnos*" (more typical in Europe). *Ethnos* can entail race, but concentrates more on ethnicity as well as cultural/ancestral heritage. This ideology views human beings through a "biocultural"[6] lens. In this perspective, human biology and human culture are closely connected. More specifically, human subgroup biology (genetic differences between ethnicities/races, among others) and different human cultures are intertwined. They are also heavily interested in issues of identity and culture, and are focused on how policies like increased immigration could (or have) fundamentally changed the identity of a nation. Note that this is not a "movement" in the usual sense, but rather a construction for our purposes that assists in providing some order to what we are describing.[7] Obviously, this description is intentionally broad, and does leave many of the nuances to the side,[8] but it will work for the purposes of this discussion. There are other sub-trends within the Alt-Right, many of which are in some conflict with each other on assumptions and ideational foundations, including "Traditionalists," followers of Julius Evola,[9] certain types of libertarians taking inspiration from the work of Hans-Herman Hoppe,[10] remaining followers of older racialist thinkers/activists like William L. Pierce[11] or George Lincoln Rockwell,[12] and various others. The "Alt-Right" obviously has numerous overlaps with elements of mainstream political conservatism, but its manner of thinking through these issues is different. Alt-Rightists primarily think in systemic ways, seeing demographic differences and changes as being paramount in the rise and fall of societies. Consider discrimination of a type as an example, specifically the debates on "critical race theory" (CRT) in American schools. Mainstream conservatives tend to argue that the problem with CRT is that it is inherently discriminatory, including to whites, but also to Asians and other groups. For Alt-Rightists, on the other hand, the problem with CRT is it is inherently anti-white (and at best secondarily discriminatory to other groups). This may seem a minor framing difference, but it also reflects fundamental differences. The mainstream conservative view is a classically liberal perspective of racial identity being a secondary (and rather inconsequential) characteristic of a rational individual, while the Alt-Right view sees racial identity as much more holistic and important, leaning to the idea that white populations should engage in the types of identity-based politics pursued by other racial/ethnic groups.

This brings us to the Intersectional Left, a tendency with which the reader will likely be less familiar by name, but more familiar in substance. This term covers a rather large grouping of people: critical race theorists, queer theorists, intersectionality theorists, third/fourth-wave feminists, indigenous activists, transgender activists, and various others.[13] As with the Alt-Right, this is a construction for clarity's sake. A unifying feature of the Intersectional Left is its dichotomy of oppressed versus oppressor, the marginalized versus the privileged. Unlike the Alt-Right, the Intersectional Left emphasizes the "social construction" of identity, as well as emphasizing the "lived experiences" and particular "ways of knowing" a population may possess. That said, the Intersectional Left tends to share a similar type of determinism as the Alt-Right. Even if identities are "constructed" through language and narratives, society is trapped within these linguistic constructions regardless of the individual's actions and intentions. A comparison with the Alt-Right might clarify the matter. For some Alt-Right forms of thinking, group-level genetic predisposition results in some populations being generally unable to operate within strict rule-of-law societies (with American Blacks being an example used).[14] This is obviously a rather deterministic view. In turning to some of the "anti-racist" literature of the Intersectional Left, however, one finds an underlying similarity. In one popular "anti-racism" text, whites who wish to "do the work" can at best merely be "anti-racist racists," but are effectively doomed by their identity to be life-long oppressors.[15] Whether by genetics or "construction," these two tendencies share a group-based notion of determinism with notable similarities to earlier totalitarian ideologies. One might wonder, looking at the types of views in the Intersectional Left, if there is anything that really connects these disparate groups other than perhaps some significant overlap in their policy preferences and voting patterns in the USA. But despite their many differences, they do have some "threads" that fundamentally connect them, just as with the Alt-Right. The underlying premise for the Intersectional Left is the dichotomy of oppressed versus oppressor (or, if one prefers, the "privileged" versus the "marginalized"), with inequitable differences of power as the main basis for these inequalities. Much of these ideas are outcroppings of notions within the "New Left," and still maintain a Hegelian/Marxian infrastructure (even if these earlier philosophies are rejected). Within this framework, the "marginalized" – whoever they may be – are allied together against the "privileged." This dynamic tends to mean that being one of the "marginalized" requires recognition from previously recognized "marginalized" groups. Moreover, the emphasis on "lived experience" evokes a notion that certain types of knowledge cannot be accessed by people who are "privileged," thus a "white cishet male" would be incapable of truly understanding the position of a Person of Color transgender lesbian, for instance. Structurally, this is rather similar to some earlier Marxian forms of argument. The denunciation of "bourgeois legality" and "bourgeois rationality" 60 years ago are now rephrased as condemnations of "white supremacist legality" or "phallogocentric rationality."

With both of these tendencies, the danger is in "percolation" into more mainstream or dominant movements and/or organizations. Note that "percolation" does not necessarily mean that such movements/organizations would quickly change and advocate for totalitarian policies. Rather, the greatest danger in "percolation" is that more mainstream/dominant groups begin *thinking along similar lines* as the totalitarian tendencies. Let's use the example of crime in the United States. The immediate danger is not that American conservatives will instantaneously shift into being "race realists," nor that American progressives will immediately start arguing that incarceration of violent criminals is merely "white supremacist"-style slavery by other means. It is instead from the subtle shift in how the issue is considered that becomes the problem. If the American Right or American Left starts thinking of crime in terms of fixed racial categories – ones with clear "good" populations and equally clear "Enemies" – then the seeds are planted for the more extreme, totalitarian ideological elements to rise. By the time these seeds fully bloom, it is usually too late to stop totalitarian advancement, since people now consider these lines of thinking as self-evident and reasonable, and changing their minds would be a daunting task. How far this "percolation" has occurred, for either or both tendencies discussed here, I leave for the reader to consider.

But I would ask the reader, especially those from the United States, to pause at this point. Think of your own beliefs, your own assumptions, and your own forms of self-identification. If you are like many Americans, you might have agreed with the summations of some of the views in this section, while vehemently disagreeing with other parts. More specifically, if you lean more toward the Left, you probably found much that was sensible in the Alt-Right discussion, but much contestable on the Intersectional Left discussion (and vice-versa for those on the Right). The question for the reader to consider is "why?" Or, more specifically, if you found yourself displeased with some of the framing of the discussion focused on your general "side" of the political spectrum, is it because the discussion was wrong (which is fully possible; while the author does have a rather elevated view of himself, he certainly is not perfect), or is it because of an unselfconscious belief that one's own side cannot possibly have totalitarian elements within it? Consider it carefully. If it is the latter, you can now see the starting point where "percolation" can develop.

It could be possible to defuse the ability of such tendencies to "percolate" into the mainstream. Perhaps the most obvious solution would be to seek depolarization within society. By creating greater unity, the society could weather future crises with less danger of totalitarian ideologies and movements gaining popularity. But how would this occur? Depolarization often occurs along one of two lines. The first – and greatly preferred – method is depolarization "organically" (for lack of a better word). Through the slow process of local and interpersonal actions, individuals within such countries can mitigate the types of isolation and anomie that mass society often creates. Through this process of finding commonalities on an interpersonal level, other differences (class, race, religion, and so forth) can be softened without needing coercion. As silly as it may sound, forming a knitting club or joining an amateur football team can depolarize better than numerous laws and regulations. The second, and significantly harsher, method is through coercion and force. Typically, this is the method that would be used by a victorious invading army against the native population, where symbols/functions related to previous loyalties are destroyed and new ones are created in their place. Obviously, this type of "depolarization" can make things much worse. Forced unification can exacerbate underlying tensions, and indeed create even more room for extreme ideologies. In polarized times, perhaps one of the most pernicious moves is to attempt a forced depolarization. Many people quite reasonably view this type of "unity" as simply being ideational imperialism. One is less than inclined to respond positively to an opponent who says, "we all just need to get beyond our differences, come together, and do everything I want." A potentially emergent form of totalitarianism does seem to use this type of passive-aggressive, "nudging" form of coercion, so, let's spend a little time talking about it.

Technocratic Totalitarianism on the Rise?

Totalitarianism historically develops from parties and movements that seek to destroy what exists and replace it with something new. Indeed, the author cannot think of a single historical instance where a totalitarian regime developed *ex nihil* within a country among its elites. Totalitarianism has come either from these parties/movements or has been imposed by an external country's military (as in the case of Eastern Europe after the Second World War). But in recent years, there is more of a concern that something new may be arising: a type of "technocratic totalitarianism," a "rule by experts" with traits of totalitarian rule.

Chapter 3 briefly mentioned technocracy, the "rule by experts," but let's expand on the notion. In its modern origins,[16] the notion of technocracy often takes on the language of engineering or science. Just as there are experts in aerodynamics or nuclear physics, so too there can be experts in social/political organization (thus the creation of the term "social engineering"). Technocratic views are generally of a different nature than that of totalitarian ideology. While totalitarians generally think in terms of "History" and the "New Society," technocrats often seem almost bureaucratic in their way of thinking, as they are focused on the minutiae of policies and the notion of "experimenting" for improved – but not perfect – societies (with the technocrats in charge, of course). That said, once a totalitarian regime has been in place for some time, it does appear that the line between vanguardist organization and technocratic organization tends to blur. Being fluent and adept in Marxism-Leninism (for instance) places an individual among the regime's "experts," and these "experts" are a part of the regime's overall single-party system. Thus far, there has been no purely technocratic system put in place as a government, so one can only speculate if a technocratic regime would start blurring into a totalitarian organization as well.

Which brings us to "technocratic totalitarianism." The following, by necessity, is quite speculative, and thus should be taken by the reader with some hesitancy. We could define "technocratic totalitarianism" as a totalitarian ideology/organization/regime that bases its legitimacy upon the knowledge/training of an "expert" class, with the view that this "expert" class – by its educational and social position – has the right, power, and duty to shift humanity toward a "New Society," and that (organizationally) emphasizes bureaucratic, regulatory, and other less-accountable parts of government/social structures to advance its views. What is different in in this form of totalitarianism is that the "world-historic" population (the "credentialed," for lack of a better term) takes pride of place in it, while the "History" upon which it is justified is of a shifting and amorphous nature. The unifying element is expertise, but "credentials" is perhaps a more accurate term. "Expertise" is determined by having the "correct" types of degrees from the "correct" types of universities, and where "expertise" arises from the consensus among other experts (rather than from an external truth or reality). In other words, one could say that "expertise" arises from consensus within the "world-historic" population, rather than "expertise" coming from a relation to reality that is independent of any other group's opinion of it. Rather than being the daring revolutionaries and terrorists of previous totalitarian movements, the technocratic totalitarian gravitates toward bureaucracy. In the realm of large, international organizations (governmental, corporate, nongovernmental, or what have you), this population can have widespread influence while maintaining bureaucratic anonymity and unaccountability. This credentialed "expert" population could in some ways be called the "laptop" class, as it seems particularly focused upon telecommunication and advanced electronic technology, and seems most adept with topics of networks, large datasets, and advanced computing. A major difference in this form, however, is the ambiguity of its ideas. The rule by the credentialed "expert" class is central, but rule toward what type of new society? Perhaps as a result of the comparatively new form of this movement, its basis often shifts. The fixation of the credentialed "expert" class has, at various points, emphasized globalization as an economic/cultural foundation of a new order, a new ecological order (be it in stopping ozone depletion, shifting away from fossil fuels in one of the various declared periods of "peak oil," or now on "net-zero emission"), and others.

Perhaps an example would be useful. Consider the events surrounding the COVID-19 pandemic, especially in various Western democratic nations. In short order, many nations imposed substantial limitations on their populations (limiting what businesses could be open, restricting freedom of movement for individual citizens, requiring citizens to have tracking apps that would monitor their location, and so forth), with many corporate entities aiding in these endeavors, be it in blocking "misinformation" (even if such information turned out to be correct, or at least arguably so), requiring vaccinations for continued employment, and the like. In most cases, the populations of these democracies had no vote on these restrictions. If there were complaints, political leaders often shifted responsibility to government entities – such as various ministries of health – which appeared as "black boxes" of unaccountability. One was to "Trust the Science," even if the restrictions seemed questionable through scientific analysis. One could view the national responses to COVID-19 as a type of "preview" of the technocratic totalitarian regime appearing less like the jack-booted thug of previous regimes, and more like a particularly dour Puritan busybody that forcibly "nudges" people into the "correct" direction.

Certainly, there have been plenty of authors arguing that many Western societies are becoming (or already are) totalitarian in nature, be it New Left gurus,[17] academic political theorists studying democracy,[18] or analyses from the Right on the "managerial revolution" and "managerial elite,"[19] among others. Many of these works may integrate into some of the critiques that arise from the Alt-Right (against "globalists") and Intersectional Left (against "neoliberalism"), among others. However, that such critiques should come from these ideological tendencies should not be reason enough to discard them for two reasons. First, it is a category error to assume that something cannot be totalitarian if it is criticized by totalitarian or totalitarian-leaning ideologies. There was no shortage of criticism (some rather insightful) in the arguments between Communists and Nazis, both of whom were totalitarian. Second, as long as one is attentive to the assumptions and styles of thinking that are being used in the criticisms, a thoughtful person can make use of these critiques to see if there are some fundamental problems within an ideology or form of social organization. For all of their faults, these types of thinkers can illuminate challenging parts of social systems about which we prefer not to think, even if the solutions offered are unacceptable.

Once again, this is a merely speculative exercise in a potential future form of totalitarianism. If a new form is arising, or if this is just a momentary transition toward something else . . . well, readers of the future will be able to tell.

Conclusion

Take some pride in yourself. You have just finished reading a somewhat dreary book on a very unpleasant topic. But let's conclude with something a little more hopeful. It is a rather natural human tendency to emphasize the bad rather than the good, which has been noted by many people, from Augustine of Hippo over a millennia ago to various psychologists today. One of the reasons for the interest in, and fascination with, totalitarianism is its sheer evil – simultaneously horrifying yet sickly attractive. But it ends. Moreover, contra Orwell's fears that totalitarianism's jackboot could stomp a human face forever, totalitarianism *must* end. At its foundations, totalitarianism is based on fiction, and falsity is fundamentally weaker than truth. Truth may be hard to see at times, and we often have many reasons to not *want* to see the truth, but truth outlasts individuals, regimes, and civilizations. No matter how cloyingly totalitarian ideology may tempt people, no matter how invigorating the rush of totalitarian movements may be, no matter the terror by which totalitarian regimes rule –eventually, the truth will bring them crashing down. Totalitarianism has its victories here and there, but in the end, Truth wins.

Summing Up

- While few fully totalitarian regimes exist today, some post-totalitarian states (such as China) could turn in totalitarian directions once again.
- The advent of the "telecommunications revolution," while providing many new avenues for exchanging information and forming connections, creates many disturbing possibilities for greater surveillance and coercion from a future totalitarian state.
- Ideological tendencies with totalitarian elements do still exist and could "percolate" into more mainstream political movements/parties, creating dynamics similar to those before the "Golden Age" of totalitarianism.
- The mixture of technological advancements with an increased focus on credentialed "expertise" could be developing toward a rather different form of totalitarianism based on more technocratic foundations.

Suggested Reading

If there is any genre in nonfiction writing that never lacks in supply, it is books attempting to predict the future. This is also true with texts that focus upon the potential rise of new (or reinvigorated past) totalitarian ideologies, movements, and regimes. For texts that can provide some assistance to the reader, consider McAdams and Castrillon (2022), Vormann and Weinman (2021), Zúquete (2018), March (2012), and Taylor (1995), among others. Most of these texts are focused on rightwing forms of extremism. Unfortunately, this is more a reflection of the fixations of academics rather than of possible threats in the future, so the reader may need to venture farther out to find broader sources. There are other works, of course, but the genre of "future-casting" is packed with texts of the "partisan" variety (discussed in Chapter 1), so the reader should maintain a skeptical eye when seeking out such texts.

Notes

1. Hollander (1998) provides some useful, earlier examples.
2. Among other sources, consider Herf (1984) as a good example.
3. Gray (2013): 657.
4. For a discussion of this issue in the United States, see Gray (2018): 152–153.
5. For instance, see Mosse (1989).
6. The term itself comes from O'Meara (2013), but is useful more generally.
7. See Gray (2022).
8. For fuller discussions on the Alt-Right, see Gray and Jordan (2018) and Hawley (2017). For a perspective ideologically inclined toward the Alt-Right, see Johnson (2018) and Shaw (2018).
9. Evola was involved in the Italian Fascist regime, and his "Traditionalism" focuses on esoteric knowledge and similar ideas. His most famous works are Evola (1995) and Evola (2002). See also Sedgwick (2004).
10. See Hoppe (2001), for instance.
11. Best known as the author of *The Turner Diaries* (see Macdonald 1980) and leader of the National Alliance; also see Griffin (2001).
12. See Simonelli (1999).
13. "Intersectional Left" is my own phrasing: see Gray (2022). Some useful works that exemplify these views, or discuss them, include Collins (2019), Hancock (2016), Moraga and Anzaldua (2015), Freire (2000), and Lorde (1984).
14. One of the most cogent discussions from this position is Levin (2005).
15. See Katz (2003).
16. For instance, see Olsen (2016).
17. Marcuse (1964).
18. Wolin (2008).
19. Burnham (1941).

Bibliography

Burnham, James. 1941. *The Managerial Revolution: What Is Happening in the World*. Westport: Greenwood Press.

Collins, Patricia Hill. 2019. *Intersectionality as Critical Social Theory*. Durham: Duke University Press.

Evola, Julius. 1995. *Revolt against the Modern World*. Guido Stucco, trans. Rochester: Inner Traditions International.

Evola, Julius. 2002. *Men among the Ruins: Post-War Reflections of a Radical Traditionalist*. Guido Stucco, trans. Michael Moynihan, ed. Rochester: Inner Traditions.

Freire, Paulo. 2000. *Pedagogy of the Oppressed*. Mary Bergman Ramos, trans. Thirtieth Anniversary Edition. New York: Continuum.

Gray, Phillip W. 2013. "Leaderless Resistance, Networked Organization, and Ideological Hegemony." *Terrorism and Political Violence* 25(5): 655–671.

Gray, Phillip W. 2018. "'The Fire Rises': Identity, the Alt-Right and Intersectionality." *Journal of Political Ideologies* 23(2): 141–156.

Gray, Phillip W. 2020. *Vanguardism: Ideology and Organization in Totalitarian Politics*. New York: Routledge.

Gray, Phillip W. 2022. "Whiteness as Resistance: The Intersectionality of the Alt-Right." In Christi van der Westhuizen and Shona Hunter (eds.), *Routledge International Handbook of Critical Studies in Whiteness*. London: Routledge, pp. 328–339.

Gray, Phillip W., and Sara R. Jordan. 2018. "Revealing the Alt-Right: Exploring Alt-Right History, Thinkers, and Ideas for Public Officials." *Public Voices* 15(2): 31–49.

Griffin, Robert S. 2001. *The Fame of a Dead Man's Deeds: An Up-Close Portrait of White Nationalist William Pierce*. No Location: 1stBooks.

Hancock, Ange-Marie. 2016. *Intersectionality: An Intellectual History*. Oxford: Oxford University Press.

Hawley, George. 2017. *Making Sense of the Alt-Right*. New York: Columbia University Press.

Herf, Jeffrey. 1984. *Reactionary Modernism: Technology, Culture, and Politics in Weimar and the Third Reich*. Cambridge: Cambridge University Press.

Hollander, Paul. 1998. *Political Pilgrims: Western Intellectuals in Search of the Good Society*. Fourth Edition. New Brunswick: Transaction Publishers.

Hoppe, Hans-Hermann. 2001. *Democracy: The God That Failed: The Economics and Politics, Democracy, and Natural Order*. London: Routledge.

Johnson, Greg, ed. 2018. *The Alternative Right*. San Francisco: Counter-Current Publishing, Ltd.

Katz, Judith H. 2003. *White Awareness: Handbook for Anti-Racism Training*. Second Revised Expanded Edition. Norman: University of Oklahoma Press.

Levin, Michael. 2005. *Why Race Matters: Race Differences and What They Mean*. Oakton: New Century Foundation.

Lorde, Audre. 1984. *Sister Outsider: Essays and Speeches*. Berkeley: Crossing Press.

Macdonald, Andrew. 1980. *The Turner Diaries*. Fort Lee: Barricade Books.

March, Luke. 2012. *Radical Left Parties in Europe*. London: Routledge.

Marcuse, Herbert. 1964. *One-Dimensional Man: Studies in the Ideology of Advanced Industrial Society*. Boston: Beacon Press.

McAdams, A. James, and Alejandro Castrillon (eds.). 2022. *Contemporary Far-Right Thinkers and the Future of Liberal Democracy*. London: Routledge.

Moraga, Cherrie, and Gloria Anzaldua (eds.). 2015. *The Bridge Called My Back: Writings by Radical Women of Color*. Fourth Edition. Albany: SUNY Press.

Mosse, George L. 1989. *The Crisis of German Ideology: Intellectual Origins of the Third Reich*. New York: Howard Fertig.

Olsen, Richard G. 2016. *Scientism and Technocracy in the Twentieth Century: The Legacy of Scientific Management*. Lanham: Lexington Books.

O'Meara, Michael. 2013. *New Culture, New Right: Anti-Liberalism in Postmodern Europe*. London: Arktos.

Sedgwick, Mark. 2004. *Against the Modern World: Traditionalism and the Secret Intellectual History of the Twentieth Century*. Oxford: Oxford University Press.

Shaw, George T., ed. 2018. *A Fair Hearing: The Alt-Right in the Words of Its Members and Leaders*. No Location: Arktos.

Simonelli, Frederick J. 1999. *American Fuehrer: George Lincoln Rockwell and the American Nazi Party*. Urbana: University of Illinois Press.

Taylor, Bron Raymond (ed.). 1995. *Ecological Resistance Movements: The Global Emergence of Radical and Popular Environmentalism*. Albany: State University of New York Press.

Vormann, Boris, and Michael D. Weinman (eds.). 2021. *The Emergence of Illiberalism: Understanding a Global Phenomenon*. New York: Routledge.

Wolin, Sheldon S. 2008. *Democracy Incorporated: Managed Democracy and the Specter of Inverted Totalitarianism*. Princeton: Princeton University Press.

Zúquete, José Pedro. 2018. *The Identitarians: The Movement against Globalism and Islam in Europe*. Notre Dame: University of Notre Dame Press.

BIBLIOGRAPHY

Adorno, T. W., Else Frenkel-Brunswik, Daniel J. Levinson, and R. Nevitt Sanford. 2019. *The Authoritarian Personality*. London: Verso.

Alexander, Yonah, and Dennis Pluchinsky (eds.). 1992. *Europe's Red Terrorists:
The Fighting Communist Organizations*. New York: Frank Cass.

Animal Liberation Front. 2011. *Underground: The Animal Liberation Front in the
1990s*. No Location: Warcry Communications.

Applebaum, Anne. 2003. *Gulag: A History*. New York: Anchor Books.

Arendt, Hannah. 1968. *The Origins of Totalitarianism*. New Addition. New York:
Harcourt, Inc.

Arendt, Hannah. 1994. *Eichmann in Jerusalem: A Report on the Banality of Evil*.
New York: Penguin Books.

Ashley, Paul. 2011. *The Complete Encyclopedia of Terrorist Organizations*. Philadelphia: Casemate.

Avineri, Shlomo. 1968. *The Social and Political Thought of Karl Marx*. Cambridge:
Cambridge University Press.

Avineri, Shlomo. 1972. *Hegel's Theory of the Modern State*. Cambridge: Cambridge University Press.

Axworthy, Michael. 2013. *Revolutionary Iran: A History of the Islamic Republic*.
Oxford: Oxford University Press.

Azrael, Jeremy R. 1966. *Managerial Power and Soviet Politics*. Cambridge: Harvard
University Press.

Azzam, Abdallah. 2008. "The Solid Base (Excerpts)." In Gilles Kepel and Jean-
Pierre Milelli (eds.), *Al-Qaeda in Its Own Words*. Pascale Ghazaleh, trans. Cambridge: Belknap Press, pp. 140–143.

Baehr, Peter. 2008. *Caesarism, Charisma, and Fate: Historical Sources and Modern
Resonances in the Work of Max Weber*. New Brunswick: Transaction Publishers.

Baynes, Norman H. (ed.). 2006. *Speeches of Adolf Hitler: Early Speeches, 1922–
1924, and Other Selections*. New York: Howard Fertig.

Ben-Ghiat, Ruth. 2001. *Fascist Modernities: Italy, 1922–1945*. Berkeley: University of California Press.

Berezin, Mabel. 1997. *Making of the Fascist Self: The Political Culture of Interwar Italy*. Ithaca: Cornell University Press.

Birstein, Vadim J. 2001. *The Perversion of Knowledge: The True Story of Soviet Science*. Cambridge: Westview Press.

Bloom, Joshua, and Waldo E. Martin, Jr. 2013. *Black Against Empire: The History and Politics of the Black Panther Party*. Berkeley: University of California Press.

Bosworth, R. J. B. 1998. *The Italian Dictatorship: Problems and Perspectives in the Interpretation of Mussolini and Fascism*. London: Arnold.

Bosworth, R. J. B. 2010. *Mussolini*. London: Bloomsbury.

Brown, Archie. 2009. *The Rise and Fall of Communism*. New York: Ecco.

Brzezinski, Zbigniew, and Carl F. Friedrich. 1956. *Totalitarian Dictatorship and Autocracy*. Cambridge: Harvard University Press.

Burge, David [iowahawk]. 2015 (November 10). "1. Identify a Respected Institution. 2. Kill It. 3. Gut It. 4. Wear Its Carcass as a Skin Suit, While Demanding Respect. #lefties." [tweet]. Retrieved from: https://twitter.com/iowahawkblog/status/664089892599631872.

Burleigh, Michael. 2000. *The Third Reich: A New History*. New York: Hill and Wang.

Burleigh, Michael, and Wolfgang Wipperman. 1991. *The Racial State: Germany 1933–1945*. Cambridge: Cambridge University Press.

Burnham, James. 1941. *The Managerial Revolution: What Is Happening in the World*. Westport: Greenwood Press.

Castro, Fidel. 2008. *The Declaration of Havana*. London: Verso.

Chamberlain, Lesley. 2007. *Motherland: A Philosophical History of Russia*. New York: Overlook/Rookery.

Chandler, David P. 1999. *Brother Number One: A Political Biography of Pol Pot*. Boulder: Westview Press.

Cheek, Timothy. 2002. *Mao Zedong and China's Revolutions: A Brief History with Documents*. Boston: Bedford/St. Martin's.

Clark, Katerina. 2011. *Moscow, the Fourth Rome: Stalinism, Cosmopolitanism, and the Evolution of Soviet Culture, 1931–1941*. Cambridge: Harvard University Press.

Cockburn, Patrick. 2015. *The Rise of the Islamic State: ISIS and the New Sunni Revolution*. London: Verso.

Codreanu, Corneliu Zelea. 2003. *For My Legionaries (The Iron Guard)*. Third Edition. York, SC: Liberty Bell Publications.

Cohn, Norman. 1970. *The Pursuit of the Millennium: Revolutionary Millenarians and Mystical Anarchists of the Middle Ages*. Revised and Expanded Edition. Oxford: Oxford University Press.

Collins, Patricia Hill. 2019. *Intersectionality as Critical Social Theory*. Durham: Duke University Press.

Conquest, Robert. 1986. *The Harvest of Sorrow: Soviet Collectivization and the Terror-Famine*. New York: Oxford University Press.

Conquest, Robert. 2008. *The Great Terror: A Reassessment*. Fortieth Anniversary Edition. Oxford: Oxford University Press.

Courtois, Stephane, Nicholas Werth, Jean-Louis Panne, Andrzej Packowski, Karel Bartosek, and Jean-Louis Margolin. 1999. *The Black Book of Communism: Crimes, Terror, Repression*. Mark Kramer, trans. Cambridge: Harvard University Press.

Crone, Patricia. 2004. *God's Rule, Government, and Islam: Six Centuries of Medieval Islamic Political Thought*. New York: Columbia University Press.

Davis, John (ed.). 1991. *The Earth First! Reader: Ten Years of Radical Environmentalism*. Salt Lake City: Peregrine Smith Book.

Dawson, Christopher. 2010. *The Crisis of Western Education*. Washington, DC: Catholic University Press of America.

De Grand, Alexander. 2004. *Fascist Italy and Nazi Germany: The 'Fascist' Style of Rule*. New York: Routledge.

Della Porta, Donatella, and Mario Diani. 2006. *Social Movements: An Introduction*. Second Edition. Malden, MA: Blackwell Publishing.

Dennis, David B. 2012. *Inhumanities: Nazi Interpretations of Western Culture*. Cambridge: Cambridge University Press.

Dikötter, Frank. 2010. *Mao's Great Famine: The History of China's Most Devastating Catastrophe, 1958–1962*. New York: Walker & Company.

Dikötter, Frank. 2013. *The Tragedy of Liberation: A History of the Chinese Revolution 1945–1957*. London: Bloomsbury.

Dikötter, Frank. 2016. *The Cultural Revolution: A People's 1962–1976*. London: Bloomsbury.

Doyle, William. 2018. *The Oxford History of the French Revolution*. Oxford: Oxford University Press.

Engels, Friedrich. 2008. *Socialism: Utopian and Scientific*. Third Edition. Atlanta: Pathfinder Press.

Euben, Roxanne L., and Muhammad Qasim Zaman (eds.). 2009. *Princeton Readings in Islamist Thought: Texts and Contexts from al-Banna to Bin Laden*. Princeton: Princeton University Press.

Evans, Richard J. 2016. *The Pursuit of Power: Europe 1815–1914*. New York: Penguin Books.

Evola, Julius. 1995. *Revolt against the Modern World*. Guido Stucco, trans. Rochester: Inner Traditions International.

Evola, Julius. 2002. *Men among the Ruins: Post-War Reflections of a Radical Traditionalist*. Guido Stucco, trans. Michael Moynihan, ed. Rochester: Inner Traditions.

Fanon, Frantz. 1963. *The Wretched of the Earth*. Constance Farrington, trans. New York: Grove Press.

Feuerbach, Ludwig. 1989. *The Essence of Christianity*. Buffalo: Prometheus Books.

Firsoc, Fridrish I., Harvey Klehr, and John Earl Haynes. 2014. *Secret Cables of the Comintern, 1933–1943*. Lynn Visson, trans. New Haven: Yale University Press.

Fitzpatrick, Sheila. 1999. *Everyday Stalinism: Ordinary Life in Extraordinary Times: Soviet Russia in the 1930s*. Oxford: Oxford University Press.

Fraenkel, Ernst. 2010. *The Dual State: A Contribution to the Theory of Dictatorship*. E. A. Shils, trans. Clark: The Lawbook Exchange, Ltd.

Freirc, Paulo. 2000. *Pedagogy of the Oppressed*. Mary Bergman Ramos, trans. Thirtieth Anniversary Edition. New York: Continuum.

Gellately, Robert. 2007. *Lenin, Stalin, and Hitler: The Age of Social Catastrophe*. New York: Vintage Books.

Gentile, Emilio. 2006. *Politics as Religion*. George Staunton, trans. Princeton: Princeton University Press.

Gerges, Fawaz A. 2016. *ISIS: A History*. Princeton: Princeton University Press.

Geyer, Michael, and Sheila Fitzpatrick (eds.). 2009. *Beyond Totalitarianism: Stalinism and Nazism Compared*. Cambridge: Cambridge University Press.

Gilbert, Martin. 1994. *The First World War: A Complete History*. New York: Henry Holt and Company.

Gleason, Abbott. 1995. *Totalitarianism: The Inner History of the Cold War*. Oxford: Oxford University Press.

Goldberg, Jonah. 2007. *Liberal Fascism: The Secret History of the American Left from Mussolini to the Politics of Meaning*. New York: Doubleday.

Gramsci, Antonio. 1971. *Selections from the Prison Notebooks of Antonio Gramsci*. Quintin Hoare and Geoffrey Nowell Smith, eds., trans. New York: International Publishers.

Gray, Phillip W. 2013. "Leaderless Resistance, Networked Organization, and Ideological Hegemony." *Terrorism and Political Violence* 25(5): 655–671.

Gray, Phillip W. 2014. "Vanguards, Sacralisation of Politics, and Totalitarianism: Category-Based Epistemology and Political Religion." *Politics, Religion & Ideology* 15(4): 521–540.

Gray, Phillip W. 2018. "'The Fire Rises': Identity, the Alt-Right and Intersectionality." *Journal of Political Ideologies* 23(2): 141–156.

Gray, Phillip W. 2020. *Vanguardism: Ideology and Organization in Totalitarian Politics*. New York: Routledge.

Gray, Phillip W. 2022. "Whiteness as Resistance: The Intersectionality of the Alt-Right." In Christi van der Westhuizen and Shona Hunter (eds.), *Routledge International Handbook of Critical Studies in Whiteness*. London: Routledge, pp. 328–339.

Gray, Phillip W., and Sara R. Jordan. 2018. "Revealing the Alt-Right: Exploring Alt-Right History, Thinkers, and Ideas for Public Officials." *Public Voices* 15(2): 31–49.

Gregor, A. James. 1979. *Italian Fascism and Developmental Dictatorship*. Princeton: Princeton University Press.

Gregor, A. James. 2000. *The Faces of Janus: Marxism and Fascism in the Twentieth Century*. New Haven: Yale University Press.

Gregor, A. James. 2005. *Mussolini's Intellectuals: Fascist Social and Political Thought*. Princeton: Princeton University Press.

Gregor, A. James. 2009. *Marxism, Fascism, and Totalitarianism: Chapters in the Intellectual History of Radicalism*. Stanford: Stanford University Press.

Gregor, A. James. 2012. *Totalitarianism and Political Religion: An Intellectual History*. Stanford: Stanford University Press.

Griffin, Robert S. 2001. *The Fame of a Dead Man's Deeds: An Up-Close Portrait of White Nationalist William Pierce*. No Location: 1stBooks.

Griffin, Roger. 1991. *The Nature of Fascism*. London: Routledge.

Griffin, Roger (ed.). 1995. *Fascism*. Oxford: Oxford University Press.

Griffin, Roger. 2007. *Modernism and Fascism: The Sense of Beginning under Mussolini and Hitler*. New York: Palgrave Macmillan.

Habermas, Jürgen. 1973. *Legitimation Crisis*. Cambridge: MIT Press.

Halberstam, Michael. 1999. *Totalitarianism and the Modern Conception of Politics*. New Haven: Yale University Press.

Hallas, Duncan. 2008. *The Comintern: A History of the Third International*. Chicago: Haymarket Press.

Hamid, Shadi. 2014. *Temptations of Power: Islamists and Illiberal Democracy in a New Middle East*. Oxford: Oxford University Press.

Hancock, Ange-Marie. 2016. *Intersectionality: An Intellectual History*. Oxford: Oxford University Press.

Hancock, Eleanor. 2008. *Ernst Röhm: Hitler's SA Chief of Staff*. New York: Palgrave Macmillan.

Harding, Neil. 1996. *Leninism*. Durham: Duke University Press.

Harding, Neil. 2009. *Lenin's Political Thought*. Chicago: Haymarket Books.

Harman, Chris. 2003. *The Lost Revolution: Germany 1918 to 1923*. Chicago: Haymarket Press.

Hawley, George. 2017. *Making Sense of the Alt-Right*. New York: Columbia University Press.

Hegghammer, Thomas (ed.). 2017. *Jihadi Culture: The Art and Social Practices of Militant Islamists*. Cambridge: Cambridge University Press.

Herf, Jeffrey. 1984. *Reactionary Modernism: Technology, Culture, and Politics in Weimar and the Third Reich*. Cambridge: Cambridge University Press.

Hibbert, Christopher. 2008. *Mussolini: The Rise and Fall of Il Duce*. New York: St. Martin's Press.

Hill, Christopher. 1975. *The World Turned Upside Down: Radical Ideas during the English Revolution*. New York: Penguin Books.

Hitler, Adolf. 1999[1927]. *Mein Kampf*. Ralph Manheim, trans. Boston: Mariner Books.

Hoffer, Eric. 1951. *The True Believer: Thoughts on the Nature of Mass Movements*. New York: Harper Perennial.

Hoffman, David L. 2011. *Cultivating the Masses: Modern State Practices and Soviet Socialism, 1914–1939*. Ithaca: Cornell University Press.

Hollander, Paul. 1998. *Political Pilgrims: Western Intellectuals in Search of the Good Society*. Fourth Edition. New Brunswick: Transaction Publishers.

Hoppe, Hans-Hermann. 2001. *Democracy: The God That Failed: The Economics and Politics of Monarchy, Democracy, and Natural Order*. London: Routledge.

Horowitz, Irving Louis. 1961. *Radicalism and the Revolt against Reason: The Social Theories of Georges Sorel with a Translation of His Essay on "the Decomposition of Marxism"*. London: Routledge.

Hunt, Lynn, and Jack R. Censer. *The French Revolution and Napoleon: Crucible of the Modern World*. London: Bloomsbury Academic.

Ingrao, Christian. 2013. *Believe & Destroy: Intellectuals in the SS War Machine*. Andrew Brown, trans. Cambridge: Polity.

Ings, Simon. 2016. *Stalin and the Scientists: A History of Triumph and Tragedy 1905–1953*. New York: Atlantic Monthly Press.

Jacobs, Ron. 1997. *The Way the Wind Blew: A History of the Weather Underground*. London: Verso.

Jensen, Richard Bach. 2014. *The Battle against Anarchist Terrorism: An International History, 1878–1934*. Cambridge: Cambridge University Press.

Johnson, Greg, ed. 2018. *The Alternative Right*. San Francisco: Counter-Current Publishing, Ltd.

Jordan, Sara R., and Eric C. Y. Ip. 2013. "Demystifying the Hermit Kingdom: The Constitution and Public Administration in North Korea." *International Review of Administrative Sciences* 79(3): 544–562.

Juergensmeyer, Mark. 2003. *Terror in the Mind of God: The Global Rise of Religious Violence*. Berkeley: University of California Press.

Kaczynski, Theodore J. 2010. *Technological Slavery: The Collected Writings of Theodore J. Kaczynski, a.k.a. "the Unabomber"*. Port Townsend: Feral House.

Kendall, Willmoore, and George W. Carey. 1995. *The Basic Symbols of the American Political Tradition*. Washington, DC: Catholic University of America Press.

Kepel, Gilles, and Jean-Pierre Milelli (eds.). 2008. *Al Qaeda in Its Own Words*. Cambridge, MA: Belknap Press.

Kershaw, Ian. 1998. *Hitler: 1889–1936: Hubris*. New York: W.W. Norton & Company.

Kershaw, Ian. 1999. "'Working Towards the Führer': Reflections on the Nature of the Hitler Dictatorship." In *The Third Reich: The Essential Readings*. Christian Leitz, ed. Malden, MA: Blackwell Publishing, pp. 233–252.

Kershaw, Ian. 2000. *Hitler: 1936–45: Nemesis*. New York: W.W. Norton & Company.

Khosrokhavar, Farhad. 2009. *Inside Jihadism: Understanding Jihadi Movements Worldwide*. London: Routledge.

Kołakowski, Leszek. 2005. *Main Currents of Marxism: The Founders, the Golden Age, the Breakdown*. P. S. Falla, trans. New York: W. W. Norton & Company.

Landry, Pierre F. 2008. *Decentralized Authoritarianism in China: The Communist Party's Control of Local Elites in the Post-Mao Era*. Cambridge: Cambridge University Press.

Lenin, V. I. 1969[1902]. *What Is to Be Done? Burning Questions of Our Movement*. New York: International Publishers.

Lenin, V. I. 1987. *Essential Works of Lenin: "What Is to Be Done?" and Other Writings*. H. M. Christman, ed. New York: Dover Publications.

Lenin, V. I. 1987[1917]. "Imperialism: The Highest Stage of Capitalism." In H. M. Christman (ed.), *Essential Works of Lenin: "What Is to Be Done?" and Other Writings*. New York: Dover Publications, pp. 178–270.

Levin, Michael. 2005. *Why Race Matters: Race Differences and What They Mean*. Oakton: New Century Foundation.

Liddick, Donald R. 2006. *Eco-Terrorism: Radical Environmental and Animal Liberation Movements*. Westport: Praeger.

Lifton, Robert Jay. 1961. *Thought Reform and the Psychology of Totalism: A Study of "Brainwashing" in China*. New York: W. W. Norton & Company.

Lifton, Robert Jay. 2017. *The Nazi Doctors: Medical Killing and the Psychology of Genocide*. Second Edition. New York: Basic Books.

Linz, Juan J. 2000. *Totalitarian and Authoritarian Regimes*. Boulder: Lynne Rienner Publishers.

Lister, Charles R. 2015. *The Syrian Jihad: Al-Qaeda, the Islamic State and the Evolution of an Insurgency*. Oxford: Oxford University Press.

Lloyd, G. E. R., ed. 1983. *Hippocratic Writings*. New York: Penguin Books.

Lorde, Audre. 1984. *Sister Outsider: Essays and Speeches*. Berkeley: Crossing Press.

Lüthi, Lorenz M. 2008. *The Sino-Soviet Split: Cold War in the Communist World*. Princeton: Princeton University Press.

Ma, Bo. 1995. *Blood and Sunset: A Memoir of the Chinese Cultural Revolution*. New York: Penguin Books.

Macdonald, Andrew. 1980. *The Turner Diaries*. Fort Lee: Barricade Books.

MacFarquhar, Roderick, and Michael Schoenhals. 2006. *Mao's Last Revolution*. Cambridge: Belknap Press.

Maher, Shiraz. 2016. *Salafi-Jihadism: The History of an Idea*. Oxford: Oxford University Press.

Mao, Tse-Tung. 1972. *Quotations from Chairman Mao*. Peking: Foreign Language Press.

Mao, Tse-Tung. 2007. *On Practice and Contradiction*. London: Verso.

March, Luke. 2012. *Radical Left Parties in Europe*. London: Routledge.

Marcuse, Herbert. 1964. *One-Dimensional Man: Studies in the Ideology of Advanced Industrial Society*. Boston: Beacon Press.

Marx, Karl. 1978a. *The Marx-Engels Reader*. Robert C. Tucker, ed. Second Edition. New York: W. W. Norton & Company.

Marx, Karl. 1978b. "Theses on Feuerbach." In *The Marx-Engels Reader*. Robert C. Tucker, ed. Second Edition. New York: W. W. Norton & Company, pp. 143–145.

McAdams, A. James, and Alejandro Castrillon (eds.). 2022. *Contemporary Far-Right Thinkers and the Future of Liberal Democracy*. London: Routledge.

McLellan, David. 2007. *Marxism after Marx*. Fourth Edition. New York: Palgrave Macmillan.

McPhee, Peter. 2016. *Liberty or Death: The French Revolution*. New Haven: Yale University Press.

Meyer, Alfred G. 1957. *Leninism*. New York: Frederick A. Praeger.

Michels, Robert. 1962. *Political Parties: A Sociological Study of the Oligarchical Tendencies of Modern Democracy*. Eden and Cedar Paul, trans. New York: Free Press.

Midlarsky, Manus I. 2013. *Origins of Political Extremism: Mass Violence in the Twentieth Century*. Cambridge: Cambridge University Press.

Miller, James. 1984. *Rousseau: Dreamer of Democracy*. New Haven: Yale University Press.

Mitchell, Richard P. 1969. *The Society of Muslim Brothers*. Oxford: Oxford University Press.

Montefiore, Simon Sebag. 2003. *Stalin: The Court of the Red Tsar*. New York: Vintage Books.

Mosse, George L. 1989. *The Crisis of German Ideology: Intellectual Origins of the Third Reich*. New York: Howard Fertig.

Motadel, David. 2014. *Islam and Nazi Germany's War*. Cambridge: Belknap Press.

Mozaffari, Mehdi. 2017. *Islamism: A New Totalitarianism*. Boulder: Lynne Rienner Publishers.

Mussolini, Benito. 2006. *My Autobiography, with "the Political and Social Doctrine of Fascism"*. Richard Washburn Child and Jane Soamers, trans. Mineola: Dover Publications.

Myers, B. R. 2011. *The Cleanest Race: How North Koreans View Themselves: And Why It Matters*. Brooklyn: Melville House.

Namkoong, Young. 1999. "Dependency Theory: Concepts, Classifications, and Criticisms." *International Area Studies Review* 2(1): 121–150.

Nasr, Vali. 2006. *The Shia Revival: How Conflicts within Islam will Shape the Future*. New York: W. W. Norton & Company.

Nation, R. Craig. 2009. *War on War: Lenin, the Zimmerwald Left, and the Origins of the Communist International*. Chicago: Haymarket Books.

Nederman, Cary J. 2000. *Worlds of Difference: European Discourses on Toleration, c. 1100–1550*. University Park: Pennsylvania State University Press.

Newton, Huey P. 1973. *Revolutionary Suicide*. New York: Penguin Books.

Newton, Huey P. 2009. *To Die for the People: The Writings of Huey P. Newton*. Toni Morrison, ed. San Francisco: City Lights Books.

Ohana, David. 2009. *The Dawn of Political Nihilism: Volume I of the Nihilist Order*. Brighton: Sussex Academic Press.

Olsen, Richard G. 2016. *Scientism and Technocracy in the Twentieth Century: The Legacy of Scientific Management*. Lanham: Lexington Books.

O'Meara, Michael. 2013. *New Culture, New Right: Anti-Liberalism in Postmodern Europe*. London: Arktos.

Orwell, George. 1981. *1984*. New York: Plume.

Pauli, Benjamin J. 2015. "Pacifism, Nonviolence, and the Reinvention of Anarchist Tactics in the Twentieth Century." *Journal of the Study of Radicalism* 9(1): 61–94.

Payne, Stanley G. 1995. *A History of Fascism, 1914–1945*. Madison: University of Wisconsin Press.

Payne, Stanley G. 2011. *Civil War in Europe, 1905–1949*. Cambridge: Cambridge University Press.

Pichot, André. 2009. *The Pure Society: From Darwin to Hitler*. David Fernbach, trans. London: Verso.

Pickering, Leslie James. 2007. *The Earth Liberation Front: 1997–2002*. Portland: Arissa Media Group.

Piekalkiewicz, Jaroslaw, and Alfred Wayne Penn. 1995. *Politics of Ideocracy*. Albany: State University of New York Press.

Pierce, William L. 2012. *Who We Are*. No Location: Revisionist Books.

Pipes, Richard. 1990. *The Russian Revolution*. New York: Vintage Books.

Qutb, Sayyid. 2002. *Milestones*. New Delhi: Islamic Book Services (P) Ptd.

Rinehart, Christine Sixta. 2013. *Volatile Social Movements and the Origins of Terrorism: The Radicalization of Change*. Lanham: Lexington Books.

Roberts, David D. 2006. *The Totalitarian Experiment in Twentieth-Century Europe: Understanding the Poverty of Great Politics*. London: Routledge.

Roberts, David D. 2020. *Totalitarianism*. Medford: Polity Press.

Robespierre, Maximilien. 2007. *Virtue and Terror*. Jean Ducange, ed. London: Verso.

Rosenberg, Alfred. 2011[1937]. *The Myth of the Twentieth Century: An Evaluation of the Spiritual-Intellectual Confrontations of Our Age*. Wentzville, MO: Invictus Books.

Rousseau, Jean-Jacques. 1984. *A Discourse on Inequality*. New York: Penguin Books.

Rousseau, Jean-Jacques. 1994. *The Social Contract*. Oxford: Oxford University Press.

Roy, Oliver, 2017. *Jihad and Death: The Global Appeal of Islamic State*. Cynthia Schoch, trans. Oxford: Oxford University Press.

Scheeres, Julia. 2012. *A Thousand Lives: The Untold Story of Jonestown*. New York: Free Press.

Schivelbusch, Wolfgang. 2006. *Three New Deals: Reflections on Roosevelt's America, Mussolini's Italy, and Hitler's Germany, 1933–1939*. New York: Picador.

Schnapp, Jeffrey T. (ed.). 2000. *Primer of Italian Fascism*. Lincoln, NE: University of Nebraska.

Schumann, Dirk. 2009. *Political Violence in the Weimar Republic, 1918–1933: Fight for the Streets and Fear of Civil War*. Thomas Dunlap, trans. New York: Berghahn Books.

Sedgwick, Mark. 2004. *Against the Modern World: Traditionalism and the Secret Intellectual History of the Twentieth Century*. Oxford: Oxford University Press.

Service, Robert. 1985. *Lenin: A Political Life: Volume I: The Strengths of Contradiction*. Bloomington: Indiana University Press.

Service, Robert. 2007. *Comrades: A History of World Communism*. Cambridge: Harvard University Press.

Service, Robert. 2009. *Trotsky: A Biography*. Cambridge: Belknap Press.

Shambaugh, David. 2007. *China's Communist Party: Atrophy and Adoption*. Washington, DC: Woodrow Wilson Center Press.

Shaw, George T., ed. 2018. *A Fair Hearing: The Alt-Right in the Words of Its Members and Leaders*. No Location: Arktos.

Shlapentokh, Vladimir. 1988. "The Stakhanovite Movement: Changing Perceptions over Fifty Years." *Journal of Contemporary History* 23(2): 259–276.

Shorten, Richard. 2012. *Modernism and Totalitarianism: Rethinking the Intellectual Sources of Nazism and Stalinism, 1945 to the Present*. London: Palgrave Macmillan.

Shorten, Richard. 2015. "Rethinking Totalitarian Ideology: Insights from the Anti-Totalitarian Canon." *History of Political Thought* 36(4): 726–761.

Siemens, Daniel. 2013. *The Making of a Nazi Hero: The Murder and Myth of Horst Wessel*. London: I. B. Tauris.

Silke, Andrew (ed.). 2019. *Routledge Handbook of Terrorism and Counterterrorism*. London: Routledge.

Simonelli, Frederick J. 1999. *American Fuehrer: George Lincoln Rockwell and the American*. Urbana: University of Illinois Press.

Smith, J., and Andre Moncourt. 2009. *The Red Army Faction: A Documentary History: Volume I: Projectiles for the People*. Oakland: PM Press.

Smith, J., and Andre Moncourt. 2013. *The Red Army Faction: A Documentary History: Volume II: Dancing with Imperialism*. Oakland: PM Press.

Snyder, Timothy. 2010. *Bloodlands: Europe between Hitler and Stalin*. New York: Basic Books.

Sorel, Georges. 2004[1950]. *Reflections on Violence*. T. E. Hulme and J. Roth, trans. Mineola: Dover Publications, Inc.

Sperber, Jonathan. 2013. *Karl Marx: A Nineteenth-Century Life*. New York: Liveright Publishing Corporation.

Stackelberg, Roderick, and Sally A. Winkle (eds.). 2002. *The Nazi Germany Sourcebook: An Anthology of Texts*. London: Routledge.

Stalin, Joseph V. 2002. *Selected Works*. Honolulu: University Press of the Pacific.

Stanley, Jason. 2018. *How Fascism Works: The Politics of Us and Them*. New York: Random House.

Sternhell, Zeev. 1994. *The Birth of Fascist Ideology: From Cultural Rebellion to Political Revolution*. David Maisel, trans. Princeton: Princeton University Press.

Stites, Richard. 1989. *Revolutionary Dreams: Utopian Visions and Experimental Life in the Russian Revolution*. New York: Oxford University Press.

Suny, Ronald Grigor. 2011. *The Soviet Experiment: Russia, the USSR, and the Successor States*. New York: Oxford University Press.

Symbionese Liberation Army. 2019. *Death to the Fascist Insect*. John Brian King, ed. No Location: Spurl Editions.

Tackett, Timothy. 2015. *The Coming of the Terror in the French Revolution*. Cambridge: Belknap Press.

Talmon, J. L. 1985. *The Origins of Totalitarian Democracy*. Cambridge: Westview Press.

Taylor, Bron Raymond (ed.). 1995. *Ecological Resistance Movements: The Global Emergence of Radical and Popular Environmentalism*. Albany: State University of New York Press.

Tucker, Robert C. 1969. *The Marxian Revolutionary Idea*. New York: W. W. Norton & Company.

Unger, Aryeh L. 1974. *The Totalitarian Party: Party and People in Nazi Germany and Soviet Russia*. Cambridge: Cambridge University Press.

Varon, Jeremy. 2004. *Bringing the War Home: The Weather Underground, the Red Army Faction, and Revolutionary Violence in the Sixties and Seventies*. Berkeley: University of California Press.

Voegelin, Eric. 1952. *The New Science of Politics: An Introduction*. Chicago: University of Chicago Press.

Walicki, Andrzej. 1995. *Marxism and the Leapt to the Kingdom of Freedom: The Rise and Fall of the Communist Utopia*. Stanford: Stanford University Press.

Warrick, Joby. 2016. *Black Flags: The Rise of ISIS*. New York: Anchor Books.

Watt, Jeffrey R. 2020. *The Consistory and Social Discipline in Calvin's Geneva*. Rochester: University of Rochester.

Weikart, Richard. 2004. *From Darwin to Hitler: Evolutionary Ethics, Eugenics, and Racism in Germany*. New York: Palgrave Macmillan.

Wiser, James L. 1980. "From Cultural Analysis to Philosophical Anthropology: An Examination of Voegelin's Concept of Gnosticism." *Review of Politics* 42(1): 92–104.

Wolin, Sheldon S. 2008. *Democracy Incorporated: Managed Democracy and the Specter of Inverted Totalitarianism*. Princeton: Princeton University Press.

Yack, Bernard. 1992. *The Longing for Total Revolution: Philosophic Sources of Social Discontent from Rousseau to Marx and Nietzsche*. Berkeley: University of California Press.

Yang, Jisheng. 2012. *Tombstone: The Great Chinese Famine 1958–1962*. New York: Farrar, Straus and Giroux.

Yang, Jisheng. 2016. *The World Turned Upside Down: A History of the Chinese Cultural Revolution*. New York: Farrar, Straus and Giroux.

Zúquete, José Pedro. 2018. *The Identitarians: The Movement against Globalism and Islam in Europe*. Notre Dame: University of Notre Dame Press.

INDEX